*"Try to say sumpin' funny, Joe."*

# KILROY WAS HERE

\* \* \* \* \* \* \* \* \* \* \* \* \* \* \* \* \* \*

## THE BEST AMERICAN HUMOR FROM WORLD WAR II

EDITED AND WITH AN INTRODUCTION BY

## CHARLES OSGOOD

HYPERION

NEW YORK

A list of permissions, constituting a continuation of the copyright page, appears on pages 187–188.

Library of Congress Cataloging-in-Publication Data

Osgood, Charles.
    Kilroy was here / [compiled] by Charles Osgood.—1st ed.
       p.    cm.
    Contents: A dictionary of American military slang, 1941-4—Boot camp—Shipping out—In the field, seas, and skies—Mess and other grub—R&R—Army vs. Navy vs. Marines vs. Air Force vs. ——Accidental insubordination and other miscellaneous occurrences in the line of duty—We have met the enemy—USO and military shows—Celebrities at the front—Looking ahead.
    ISBN 0-7868-6661-6
    1. World War, 1939-1945—Humor. 2. United States. Army—Military life. 3. American wit and humor. I. Title.
D745.2.O84    2001
940.53—dc21      00-054163

Paperback ISBN 0-7868-8574-2

*Book design by Casey Hampton*

FIRST PAPERBACK EDITION

10  9  8  7  6  5  4  3

*Kilroy Was Here* is dedicated to all the Americans in uniform during the war, whether on land, at sea, or in the air; in Europe, the Pacific, or here at home. Wherever they served during those years, whatever role they played, they were part of a great and historic undertaking that saved the world for the rest of us, nothing less. The fact that they did so without losing their sense of humor makes their achievement all the more awesome. We can never thank them enough.

# CONTENTS

# INTRODUCTION

It's a combat scene in a war movie. Dogface infantrymen digging in, with the battle sounds of shells and grenades exploding around them and bullets whizzing overhead. The field telephone rings and a helmeted GI reaches for it, picks up the receiver, and answers: "World War TWO!"

We laugh because it's so incongruous. The soldier was supposed to be in the middle of the war, sure, but that's not the way field phones were answered, of course. Yet there is some truth in it. The war was indeed on a worldwide scale, touching virtually everyplace and everybody on the planet in one way or another. Yet for each individual, the war was where he or she was at that moment. And in the case of soldiers, sailors, marines, and airmen in combat, there was the reality that any moment could be their last.

So when we think of the Second World War, the word "humor" is not exactly the first thing that springs to mind. It was a deadly serious, murderously grim business. Millions sacrificed life, limb, home, family, everything. General William

Tecumseh Sherman's saying "War is hell" fits World War II perfectly.

Yet it would not be true to say there was nothing funny about it. The war was a tragicomic mixture of the banal and the heroic, of the obscene and the absurd. There have been brilliantly comedic books, plays, and movies about that period in history. I think of Charlie Chaplin's film *The Great Dictator*, Jack Benny's *To Be or Not to Be*, remade more recently by Mel Brooks, and of Joseph Heller's classic novel *Catch 22*, which also became a movie, to cite just a few examples.

Television, from its earliest days, found humor in soldiering. *Sgt. Bilko*, with Phil Silvers, was one of TV's first hits. And then there was *Hogan's Heroes*. Being a POW in a German camp cannot possibly have been as amusing as it seemed on that television series. In fact, there were many viewers who were offended by the whole premise: Deep down Colonel Klink and Sergeant Schultz were not such bad guys when you got to know them. We know this was not the way of things in real Nazi prison camps.

But humor and laughter are a part of life, a part of being human. Even in the grimmest of times, people find things to laugh about. Gallows humor is not uncommon in newsrooms, where I've spent my whole professional life and where disaster, natural and man made, is the stock in trade. It's not only because we journalists are cynical, insensitive louts, although that is one possible explanation for it. I think it's more likely that there's a fine line between tragedy and comedy, between tears and laughter.

The hard-won victory over Nazi Germany and Imperial Japan came at enormous cost, but it saved the world from unspeakable evil. This was the good war, the just war. It was a war we had to win. "We can, we will, we must!" was the slogan. Our Allies were fighting for their lives. America was fighting for its life, too. In spite of that, there was humor. There was laughter.

We have a need to laugh even in such unfunny times and circumstances. The more fearsome and threatening the situation, the more we need a sense of humor to keep going and hold on to our sanity. A lot of the jokes were about the platoon sergeant, the company commander, the cook and the chow he turned out. And SPAM. The kind of SPAM that predated the Internet.

And, of course, there was endless kidding about sex. We have to remember that most of our "boys in uniform" were indeed boys—seventeen, eighteen, nineteen years old. Some even younger. Yes, some of them lied about their age, not to keep out of the service, but to get in, strange as that may seem to those more familiar with the Vietnam era. Boys will be boys. And they joked about what they thought about all the time and talked about all the time, which of course was sex.

Although I was alive throughout World War II, I was too young to serve. If I had lied about my age, they wouldn't have believed me anyway. The United States went into the war when I was eight. My sister Mary Ann was about to turn eight also. We were "Irish twins." I was born on January 8, 1933, and she was born December 20 of that same year.

When we were in the third and fourth grades at Our Lady of Lourdes school in Baltimore, we went to a fund-raising show one Sunday afternoon at the Roman Catholic church attached to the school. Actually the school was attached to the church, but we always thought of it the other way around. This particular Sunday happened to be December 7, 1941. ("A date that will live in infamy" as President Roosevelt would later describe it.)

Anyway, right in the middle of the show, out onto the stage came the church sexton to inform everybody that there was awful news on the radio. The Japanese had attacked our U.S. naval base at Pearl Harbor. My sister and I could tell right away that this must not be part of the show because nobody laughed or applauded. People gasped.

When we got home, we told our parents. They hadn't heard the news, so we turned on the radio. Sure enough, there it was. The radio, from the very beginning, was how we kept in touch with the world at war—through the distinctive voices of Ed Murrow, Lowell Thomas, Robert Trout, Gabriel Heatter, H. V. Kaltenborn, and others. From then on, it was all war news. Everything else seemed trivial and unimportant.

After the war news, we would listen to variety shows with war songs like "Praise the Lord and Pass the Ammunition," "Don't Sit Under the Apple Tree with Anyone Else but Me," and ditties like the Spike Jones song with the memorable chorus: "Ven Der Fuhrer Says Vee Iss der Master Race vee go Heil! (SNORT) Heil! (SNORT) Right in der Fuhrer's Face!" What I transcribed as "snort" is best performed with what some call a "raspberry."

Also keeping up our spirits on the home front were radio stars like Jack Benny, Fred Allen, Red Skelton, Fanny Brice, and Abbott and Costello. Most of their material was war related, too: jokes about war bonds and ration coupons, scrap drives, and bringing your fat can into the butcher shop. The "fat can" was not an anatomical reference. It was about saving the fat rendered from bacon or any other meat, which could somehow be used in the making of munitions.

Everything concerned the war. The bad guys on the radio serial dramas weren't thieves and murderers anymore. They were Axis spies. Just a week after the bombing of Pearl Harbor, on one of my favorite shows, *The Green Hornet*, the Hornet's faithful Japanese servant, Kato, suddenly became a faithful *Filipino* servant. No explanation given, none required.

So the Second World War is not just something out of the history books for me. It is a strong memory. What I remember most about the war is that everything else besides the war was put on hold. Time itself was referred to not as Standard or Daylight Saving Time, but as "War Time." Baltimore streets still had gaslights in those days. I remember during blackouts and air-raid drills going out to the streetlight in front of our house and pulling the chain to put out the gaslight. There were never any actual air raids, just drills and blackouts. We mainland Americans were very lucky in that regard. The sirens would simply mean another drill, never that bombs were about to start falling on us.

I remember food and gasoline rationing, salvaging anything metal, and Dad taking a second job as an expeditor (whatever that was) at a defense plant. I also remember, with pleasure, our Victory Garden in the backyard. We grew tomatoes, radishes, and a couple of other vegetables. But what really sticks in my mind is one extremely large pumpkin, which we took to school and for which we got some sort of prize. How this great pumpkin (or the radishes or tomatoes) contributed in any way to the Allied war effort I'm not quite sure. But we won, didn't we? I'm sure that pumpkin of ours must have scared the hell out of the Axis powers.

The war was so much the center of everything in those days that when I was a paperboy and delivered the *Baltimore Sun* to homes in our neighborhood, I remember wondering what in the world the newspapers were going to write about once the war was over. Every front-page story was about some aspect of how the war was going in Europe and in the Pacific.

They used to say there are no atheists in foxholes. This may or may not be true. But there certainly were comedians in the foxholes. Many soldiers recount that there was always somebody with a wisecrack or gesture of some sort. Anything to get a laugh and break the tension. But most of the humor is elusive now. You had to be there, in the boot camps, in training exercises, on the troopships and on maneuvers, even in combat to have experienced it. It wasn't just when Bob Hope or some other star came around to cheer up the troops that there was laughter. In between the professional entertainers, the troops made their own jokes, kidded each other, and joked incessantly about their situation. So much of it was of the moment.

Most elusive and yet ubiquitous of all was our friend Kilroy. He is the little bald-headed character, an American soldier presumably, peering over the fence with the message I've used as the title of this book. "Kilroy Was Here" was a running gag throughout the war. There he was on the torch of the Statue of Liberty. There he was on a girder of the George

Washington Bridge. There he was on the Arc de Triomphe in Paris, on the Marco Polo Bridge in China. One story has it that in Potsdam, Germany, in July 1945, during a meeting of the "Big Three," the Soviet Union's Josef Stalin came running out of a marble bathroom off limits to all but him, British Prime Minister Clement Atlee, and President Harry S. Truman, the Big Three themselves. Stalin was clearly agitated and conferring urgently with his aides. A translator heard him ask "Who is Kilroy?"

I'm told that there was indeed a Kilroy. His name was James J. Kilroy and he was a civilian, a welding inspector at the Bethlehem Steel shipyard in Quincy, Massachusetts. (My Aunt Maude was teaching school there in Quincy at the time.) Most inspectors used to mark the work they inspected and approved with a little chalk. But James J. Kilroy wanted them to know, in the case of the work he approved, that he was the one who did the approving—so he wrote it out in crayon on each one: "Kilroy Was Here . . ." That started it. It spread from that shipyard in Quincy across the country and around the world. A repairman in a far-off dock in some remote port would open up a space behind a bulkhead or under the deck to get something that needed fixing. And there it would be, "Kilroy" in some sealed compartment where theoretically no one had ever been before. The graphic that went with it, the little drawing of the bald-headed character peering over a fence, is apparently based on a British cartoon character named, believe it or not, "Mr. Chad." No relation to any chads, dimpled, hanging, pregnant, or otherwise, that may have appeared in the news in more recent times. To me, the amazing thing about Kilroy is that the joke, graphic and all, spread into nooks and crannies here at home and around the world without anyone organizing or manipulating it. No government propaganda pushing it. No ad agency behind it. It just happened, a joke that everybody was in on. (Except Joe Stalin, apparently.)

I once asked the late Steve Allen, the gifted musician and comedian who was the first host of NBC's *The Tonight Show*, if he could explain to me what it is that makes something funny. He told me he'd thought about that a lot but could not quite define it. He suspected it had something to do with surprise and with recognition. But to break it down or analyze it beyond that, said Allen, was like trying to analyze a sunset. You could reduce the colors of a sunset to numbers representing differing rates of refraction along the spectrum of light, but that wouldn't tell you anything about why we humans think it's beautiful. The same with music. We could learn everything there is to know about quavers and demi-quavers, audio frequencies and amplitude, and we still wouldn't understand why an aria by Puccini brings tears to our eyes.

There was a news story about a radiologist at the University of Rochester Medical School who has made a study of the laughter mechanisms in the brain. I contacted Dr. Dean Shibata to ask him the same question I had asked Steve Allen. He told me about three specific areas of the brain. The first is just above your right eye. It's called the ventral frontal lobe. The second is near the top of your head. That's the supplemental motor area. And the third is a part of the base of your brain called the nucleus incumbent. (That sounds like a political job, doesn't it?)

Dr. Shibata believes these three parts of the brain work together to trigger the laughter response when something unexpected or abnormal interferes with normal perceptions. He thinks laughter may have evolved as a way of coping with highly negative emotions by providing a quick, positive, highly pleasurable one. It also communicates this to those around us. Laughter is contagious, reassuring, and even protective. "Everything is going to be okay, it tells us. This won't really kill us." Dr. Shibata says when things get so threatening that no laughter is possible, our responses freeze into post-traumatic stress syndrome, or "shell shock," as it was called in World War I, a war that was also known in its time as "The War to End All Wars." (It obviously didn't end all wars or you wouldn't be holding a book about the humor of World War II!)

But knowing the mechanisms and parts of the brain involved in laughter doesn't tell you about what funniness is or how it feels to laugh anymore than some biological explanation can tell you how it feels to be in love. Some people can tell a joke and make others laugh and some can't. You either "get it" or you don't. All the explaining in the world will not make you laugh if you didn't laugh in the first place.

So you will not find a lot of analysis or explanation in this book. We've left the humor as it was. It speaks for itself. But I do think the humor of the day does shed some light on the people themselves and how they reacted to the things that were going on around them. They were not in the service for some limited tour of duty. They were in for "the duration." They understood that they could not go home and pick up the threads of their personal lives until the war was won. A generation of young Americans put their lives on the line, not because they wanted to be heroes, but because there was no alternative. And they did it with a typically American spirit. They joked and kidded each other even though they knew perfectly well what was at stake. Some of the things that seemed hilarious to them at the time may not seem so amusing to us in the here and now. You had to be there. But there is no mistaking the dedication and the bravery they displayed. These were gallant folk.

Ten years after the end of the war, I did my own stint in the U.S. Army. I was RA (Regular Army), serving in the United States Army Band in Washington, D.C. There I learned the song that infantrymen in training (the "walking pride of Uncle Sam") used to sing:

> *I wouldn't give a bean.*
> *To be a fancy pants Marine.*
> *I'd rather be a dogfaced soldier like I am . . .*
> *On every poster that I read it says the Army builds men*
> *So they're tearing me down to build me over again.*

They're the ones I was thinking about when I wrote the lyrics for the trio section of John Casavas's march:

GALLANT MEN

> *Gallant men have built us a nation*
> *Passed us a torch of flame.*
> *Let us hold it high and light up the sky*
> *With praise of our Gallant men.*

—*Charles Osgood*

# KILROY WAS HERE

# A DICTIONARY OF AMERICAN MILITARY SLANG

## 1941–1944

From the appendix to *Gone With the Draft: Love Letters of a Trainee*, by Park Kendall (M. S. Mill Co., Inc., 1941) and *More G.I. Laughs: Real Army Humor*, selected by Harold Hersey (Sheridan House, 1944)

**A.B.** area bird; cadet walking punishment tours in area of barracks

**AFRICAN GOLF** crap shooting

**ALBATROSS** chicken

**ARMORED COW** canned milk

**ARMY BANJO** shovel

**ARMY STRAWBERRIES** prunes

**AWKWARD SQUAD** where backward rookies receive elementary instruction

**B-ACHE** complaint, or to complain [bellyache]

**BARB WIRE GARTERS** imaginary . . . awarded as a consolation in lieu of medals or citations

**A BARRAGE** a party where a jug is produced and the spirited contents trickle musically into the glasses

**A BEARDED LADY**  a searchlight that diffuses

**BARRACKS FATIGUE**  loafing in quarters

**BATTERY ACID**  coffee

**BEAM, FLYING THE IRON**  pilot following railroad track

**BEAM, FLYING THE WET**  pilot following river

**BEANS**  commissary officer

**BEHAVIOR REPORT**  letter to a girl

**BELLY ROBBER**  mess sergeant

**BEND THE THROTTLE**  to fly plane or drive vehicle above normal speed

**BIG JOHN**  recruit

**BIRD DOGGING**  lower classman dancing with upper classman's girl

**BISCUIT GUN**  imaginary appliance for shooting food up to pilots who are having difficulty landing

**BLACK STRAP**  coffee

**BLACK WEDNESDAY**  calisthenics with rifles

**BLANKET DRILL**  sleep

**BLISTERFOOT**  infantryman

**BLITZ IT**  polish it

**BLOOD**  ketchup

**BOB-TAIL**  dishonorable discharge

**BOG POCKET**  tightwad

**BOODLE**  candy, cake, ice cream

**BOOTLEG**  coffee

**BOUDOIR**  squad tent

**BOWLEGS**  cavalrymen

**BRASS HAT**  staff officer

**BRASS POUNDER**  radio telegrapher

**BUBBLE DANCING**  dishwashing

**BUCKING FOR SECTION 8** seeking discharge for military ineptitude (not grounds for dishonorable discharge)

**A BUDDY** anybody anywhere who will loan you anything

**BUDDY SEAT** motorcycle sidecar

**BUGS** any solids found in soup

**BULL PEN** military prison yard

**BURN AND TURN** game of blackjack

**BUTT** cigarette

**BUTTON CHOPPER** laundry

**BUZZARD MEAT** chicken or turkey

**CAMEL CORPS** infantry (also called foot sloggers and gravel crushers)

**CANS** headphone

**CANTEEN SOLDIER** one who wears non-regulation clothing or insignia

**CAPTAIN OF THE HEAD** latrine orderly on Mine Planter

**CARP** to complain

**CARRYING A HEAVY LOAD** fatigued or melancholy

**CAT BEER** milk

**CHEESE TOASTER** bayonet (also known as cat stabber, pig sticker, toad sticker, and toothpick)

**CHEST HARDWARE** medals (also called gongs)

**CHICAGO ATOMIZER** automatic rifle

**CHILI BOWL** regulation hair cut

**CHINA CLIPPER** dishwasher

**CHINESE LANDING** one wing low

**CHOW HOUNDS** men always at head of mess line

**CITS** civilian clothing

**THE CLARA** the all-clear air raid signal. RAF.

**CLUTCH, SLIPPING THE** criticizing

**COCKPIT FOG**  mentally lost

**COFFEE COOLER**  one who seeks easy jobs

**COMPANY STOOGE**  company clerk

**COPENHAGEN**  chewing snuff

**THE CORPSE**  affectionate term for corps

**COSMOLINES**  artillery

**COUSIN**  close friend

**CRAB**  chronic complainer

**CRASH TAG**  identification bracelet

**CREAM ON SHINGLE**  creamed beef on toast

**CROOT**  recruit, also known as rookie, trainee, draftee, selectee, bimbo, bozo, dude, john, dogface, bucko, and poggie

**CROW**  chicken

**CRUMB HUNT**  kitchen inspection

**DAWN PATROLLING**  arising before reveille

**DECK MONKEYS**  deck crew of Army Mine Planter

**DEVIL'S PIANO**  machine gun

**DIDDIE BAG**  where soldier keeps valuables

**DIHEDRAL OIL**  imaginary substance which recruits are sent to procure

**DING HOW**  everything okay

**DIS**  discipline

**DIT DA ARTIST**  radio operator

**DODO**  air cadet before he's made a solo flight

**DOG FACE**  enlisted man

**DOG FAT**  butter

**DOG ROBBER**  orderly

**DOG SHOW**  foot inspection

**DOPES OFF**  acts stupidly

**DOUGH PUNCHER**  Army baker

**DRAPED**  intoxicated

**DRIVE IT IN THE HANGAR**  stop talking

**DRIVE UP**  come here

**DUFF**  any sweet edible

**EGG IN YOUR BEER**  too much of a good thing

**ELEPHANT**  cadet taking dancing lessons

**EMBALMED MEAT**  canned meat

**FILEBONER**  one striving to get ahead

**FIRST GRADER**  Master Sergeant

**FIRST MAN**  First Sergeant

**FLASH GUN**  machine gun used for training

**FLEA BAG**  your mattress

**FLYING BOXCAR**  a bomber

**FOOT SLOGGER**  an infantryman

**FRENCH LEAVE**  unauthorized absence

**FROG STICKER**  bayonet

**FUNERAL GLIDE**  plane out of control

**G-2**  inquisitiveness

**GALVANIZED GELDING**  tank

**GAS HOUSE**  a beer joint

**GAS HOUSE GANG**  chemical warfare instructors

**GASOLINE COWBOY**  member of the armored force

**GEESE**  bombers in formation

**GENERAL'S CAR**  a wheelbarrow

**A GERTRUDE**  a soldier on office duty

**GETTING THE LEMONADE**  getting eliminated or dismissed

**GET EAGER**  to strive to the utmost

**G.I. SKY PILOT**  chaplain

**GLAMOUR BOY**  draftee, selective service trainee

**GLUE**  money

**GOLDBRICK**  one who gets by without doing his share of work

**HE HAS GONE ON THE TACK** forsworn alcoholic beverages

**GNOME** member of second battalion

**GOAT** junior officer in post, regiment, etc.

**GOATY** awkward, ignorant

**GOLDFISH** canned salmon

**GOOD TILL THE LAST DROP** a parachute jumper

**GOON** soldier who falls in the lowest category in Army classification tests

**GOT IT ON THE JAWBONE** on credit

**GRASS** salad or vegetable

**GRAVEL AGITATOR** infantryman

**GRAY GHOST** the stage commander's airplane, so named because it is the last plane one rides in before being "washed out"—eliminated from flight training

**GREASE** butter

**GRINDERS** teeth

**GUARDHOUSE LAWYER** a person who knows little but talks much about regulations, military law, and "soldiers' rights"

**GUN THE POTATOES!** Might I trouble you for the potatoes?

**HALT AND FREEZE** assume position of attention

**HAM SHACK** amateur radio station or building

**HARD ROLLED** packaged cigarettes

**HASHBURNER** cook

**HAY BURNER** horse or mule

**HEDGE HOP** a short flight

**HELL BUGGY** tank

**HERDBOUND** soldier or animal unfit for further military duty

**HIGHER THAN A GEORGIA PINE** unduly excited

**HIT THE SILK** use a parachute

**HOBO** Provost Marshal

**HOMING DEVICE**  a pass or furlough

**IN A STORM**  excited

**INVISIBLE PAINT FOR CAMOUFLAGE**  here we go again . . . a
   rookie's merry-go-round

**IRISH GRAPES**  potatoes

**IRON HORSES**  tanks

**IRON PONIES**  motorcycles

**HE'S JAMMY**  very lucky

**HE'S JEEPY**  not quite all there

**JUICE JERKER**  electrician

**KEEPS DAINTY**  well-behaved

**KEEP YOUR NOSE DOWN ON THE TURNS**  take it easy

**KIP**  bed

**KIWI**  a non-flying commissioned officer of the Air Corps

**HE'S A BIT LACY**  girlish

**LANDING GEAR**  legs

**A LATRINE RUMOR**  an unsubstantiated tale

**LAYING THEIR EGGS**  bombers at work

**A LEATHERNECK**  a Marine

**LET HER EAT**  drive at full speed

**LIMP LINE**  men reporting at Sick Call

**PASS LOT'S WIFE**  the salt

**LOW ON AMPS AND VOLTAGE**  lacking ambition and ideas

**A MAE WEST**  a buoyant lifesaving jacket that slips on like a
   vest . . . and . . . well, you get the idea

**MAGGIE'S DRAWERS**  red flag used on rifle range to indicate
   a miss

**MARFAK**  butter

**MEAT WAGON**  ambulance

**MECHANICAL RATS**  two-way loudspeaker system connecting
   barrack sleeping quarters with non-coms' room

**MICE** small balls of lint on the floor

**MITT FLOPPER** a soldier who does favors for his superiors, or salutes unnecessarily; a "yes man"

**MOLE HOLE** photographic dark room

**THE MONA** moaning of an air raid alarm

**MONKEY CLOTHES** full dress uniform

**MOTHER MCCREA** a sob story

**MOTORIZED FOOTLOCKER** Bantam car

**MOTORIZED FRECKLES** insects

**NORTH DAKOTA RICE** hot cereal

**ALL PACKED UP** dead

**A PANHANDLER** hospital orderly

**PARING KNIFE** bayonet

**PARTED HIS TEETH** scored a bull's eye

**PEARL DIVER** kitchen police

**PICK UP YOUR BRASS** get out of the way

**PILLOW PIGEONS** bed bugs

**PINEAPPLE** hand grenade

**POCKET LETTUCE** currency

**POLISHING THE APPLE** flattering your superiors

**POOP SHEET** drill schedule or any written announcement

**POPEYE** spinach

**POUR ON THE COAL** give it the throttle

**PUNK** bread

**RAIN ROOM** bath house

**RED LEG** artilleryman

**REGIMENTAL MONKEY** the drum major

**RIDING THE SICK BOOT** feigning illness

**ROLL UP YOUR FLAPS** stop talking

**ROLLINGS** cigarette tobacco

**SALVA** butter

**SAND AND SPECKS**  salt and pepper

**SAWBONE**  doctor

**SEAGULL**  chicken

**SEE THE CHAPLAIN**  stop grousing

**SERUM**  intoxicating beverages

**SEWER TROUT**  whitefish

**SHACK MAN**  married man

**SHACK RAT**  garrison soldier who has made a friend in the
city and usually goes to town every night

**SHIVERING LIZ**  Jell-O again

**SHORT CIRCUIT BETWEEN THE EARPHONES**  a mental lapse

**SHOOT A LINE**  boasting

**SHOW TENT**  motion picture theater

**PASS THE SHRAPNEL**  Grape Nuts

**SHUTTERS**  sleeping pills

**SIDEARMS**  cream and sugar

**SIDE MEAT**  well pleased

**SKIRT PATROL**  search for feminine companionship

**SKY SCOUT**  chaplain

**A SLACKER**  a pal who won't entertain another girl so you
can be alone with your girlfriend

**SLAPJACKS**  pancakes

**SLUM**  stew

**SLUM BURNER**  cook

**SLUM GULLION**  hash

**SNORE SACK**  sleeping bag

**SOAP SUDS ROW**  NCOs' living quarters and area—so called
because their wives do their own laundry

**S O S**  same old stew

**SOW BELLY**  bacon

**STAG**  sentry duty

**A SPIGGOTY** a native of the banana countries—"me no spig-goty eengleesh"

**SPIN IT** retire

**STARTS TO SPOIL** intoxicated

**TO STICK YOUR NOSE IN THE TROUGH** to dine

**A SUBMARINE** a bedpan

**A SUGAR REPORT** letter from the girlfriend

**SWANKS** a soldier's best clothes

**TO SWEAT** to expect

**TAILOR MADES** factory-made cigarettes

**TAXI UP** come here

**TIGER MEAT** beef

**TIN HAT** steel helmet

**TOUGH ROW OF BUTTONS TO SHINE** hard job

**UNCLE SAM'S PARTY** payday

**WALKING DANDRUFF** cooties (also known as seam squirrels)

**WING HEAVY** inebriated

---------------------------★---------------------------

From *See Here, Private Hargrove*, by Marion Hargrove (Henry Holt, 1942)

The term "buck private" was explained to us this afternoon. It refers to the old Army game, "Pass the Buck." The sergeant is first called on the carpet for a mistake in his platoon. The sergeant seeks out the corporal and gives him a dressing-down. The corporal passes the buck by scalding the ears of the private. The private doesn't even have a mule to kick, so he can't pass the buck any farther. He keeps it. And that makes him a buck private....

# BOOT CAMP

From *See Here, Private Hargrove*, by Marion Hargrove (Henry Holt, 1942)

If First Sergeant Clarence A. Goldsmith, back in the old battery where I was supposed to have learned the art of cooking for the Army, ever gets his hands on this, it will provide him with amusement throughout a long, hard winter.

When he reads that Private Edward Thomas Marion Lawton Hargrove, ASN 34116620, is giving advice to prospective soldiers, his derisive bellow will disturb the training program in the next regiment.

"My God!" he will roar. "Look who's learning who how to do what! My God! The blind leading the blind!"

It was once said, Sergeant Goldsmith, by the eminent vegetarian George Bernard Shaw that he who can, does; he who can't, teaches.

This, dear Sergeant, is my contribution to the Army and

to posterity. Please go away and leave us young people to our studies.

If I were giving advice to the boys who have already been called into the Army and will go away in a few days, I'd sum it all up in this: "Paint the town red for the rest of your civilian week. Pay no attention to the advice that is being poured into your defenseless ears for twenty-four hours a day. Form no idea of what Army life is going to be like. Leave your mind open!"

Two weeks from now, you will be thoroughly disgusted with your new job. You will have been herded from place to place, you will have wandered in nakedness and bewilderment through miles of physical examination, you will look upon privacy and individuality as things you left behind you in a golden civilian society.

Probably you will have developed a murderous hatred for at least one sergeant and two corporals. You will write and fume under what you consider brutality and sadism, and you will wonder how an enlightened nation can permit such atrocity in its army. Take it easy, brother; take it easy.

Keep this one beam of radiant hope constantly before you: The first three weeks are the hardest.

For those first three—or possibly four—weeks, you will bear the greatest part of the painful process of adjusting yourself to an altogether new routine. In those first three weeks you will get almost the full required dose of confusion and misery. You will be afraid to leave your barracks lest the full wrath of the War Department fall upon you. You will find yourself unbelievably awkward and clumsy when you try to learn the drills, and the knowledge of this awkwardness will make you even more awkward. Unless you relax, you can be very unhappy during those first three weeks.

When you are assigned to your basic training center, you'll really get into it. You'll drill and drill, a little more each day, and when the sergeant tries to correct or advise you, you'll want to tear his throat out with your bare hands. You'll be sick of the sound of his voice before an hour has passed. The only comfort I can give you is the knowledge that the poor sergeant is having a helluva time, too. He knows what you're thinking and he can't do anything about it.

You'll be inoculated against smallpox, typhoid, tetanus, yellow fever, pneumonia, and practically all the other ills that flesh is heir to. You'll be taught foot drill, the handling of a rifle, the use of the gas mask, the peculiarities of military vehicles, and the intricacies of military courtesy. You'll be told to take your beds into the battery street for airing and then, in four or five minutes, you'll be told to bring them inside again.

Most of what you are taught will impress you as utterly useless nonsense, but you'll learn it.

You'll be initiated into the mysteries of the kitchen police, probably before you've been in the Army for a week. Possibly two days later, you'll be sent on a ration detail to handle huge bundles of groceries. You'll haul coal and trash and ashes. You'll unpack the rifles that are buried in heavy grease and you'll clean that grease off them. You'll stoke fires, you'll mop floors, and you'll put a high polish on the windows. You'll wonder if you've been yanked out of civilian life for This.

All your persecution is deliberate, calculated, systematic.

It is the collegiate practice of hazing, applied to the grim and highly important task of transforming a citizen into a soldier, a boy into a man. It is the Hardening Process.

You won't get depressed; you won't feel sorry for yourself. You'll just get mad as hell. You'll be breathing fire before it's over.

Believe me or not, at the end of that minor ordeal, you'll be feeling good. You'll be full of spirit and energy and you will have found yourself. You'll start to look around and you'll see things to make you proud. You'll find that, although your corporals and sergeants still tolerate no foolishness on the drill field or in the classes, they're good fellows when you take a break or when the day is over.

You'll look at the new men coming in to go through the same hardening period, and you'll look at them with a fatherly and sympathetic eye. They will be "rookies" to you, a veteran of almost a month.

For practical advice, there is none better than the golden rule of the Army: "Keep your eyes open and your mouth shut."

At first, you'll be inclined to tremble at the sight of every corporal who passes you on the street. You might even salute the first-class privates. Then, when the top sergeant neglects to beat you with a knout and rub GI* salt into the wounds, you might want to go to the other extreme. This way madness lies.

Let an old wound-licker beg you, from the bottom of his

---

*These two letters are the cornerstone of your future Army vocabulary. They stand for the words "Government Issue" and just about everything you get in the Army will be GI. Even the official advice.

heart and the dregs of his bitter experience, never to walk up to a corporal you've known for three or four days, slap him heartily on the back, and ask him if that was him coming in drunk at three o'clock this morning.

When corporals and sergeants are to be dealt with, always remember this: Make friendships first and leave the joking until later. When it's the top sergeant, it might be best to leave the joking permanently.

It can be very easy to start your military life on the wrong foot by giving your officers and noncommissioned officers the impression that you're a wise guy, a smart aleck. Soldiers, like senators, "don't like for a new guy to shoot his mouth off."

So much for the don'ts. On the "do" side, the most important thing for you to watch is your attitude. As a matter of straight and practical fact, the best thing that you can do is to reason that you are going into a new job. The job is temporary, but while you have it it's highly important.

As, when you go into a new job in civil life, you do your damnedest to impress your employer with your earnestness, your diligence, your interest in your work—go thou and do likewise in the Army. As in your civilian job, the impression is made in the first few weeks. You make that impression, starting from the very first day, by learning as quickly as you can, by applying yourself with energy to each task, no matter how small or how unpleasant it is. You don't get anywhere by buying soda pop or beer for your sergeant.

The one place where your attitude toward your new life will show up most clearly is in the traditional salute to an officer. He can see more in that simple gesture than in anything else you do. If your hand approaches your brow indolently, as if lifted by the breeze, he knows that you still begrudge your sacrifice or that you don't give a damn. Snap it up there.

During your first three or four weeks in the Army, you'll hear a lot of griping. You'll be doing a lot of it yourself. Gripe if you must—the Army recognizes its value as an emotional cathartic—but remember that there's a time and a place for it. Don't be unpleasant about your griping and don't get a reputation as a constant griper.

You can stay out of a lot of trouble by remembering that you are no longer governed by civil law. Your new law, the Articles of War, are important, but you don't have to study it or worry about unconsciously breaking some obscure article. The Articles of War are a matter of common sense. But, if you don't like them, writing home or to your congressman won't automatically change them.

The main things to remember are these: Watch your attitude, do your work, respect your superiors, try to get along with your fellow soldiers, keep yourself and your equipment clean at all times, and behave yourself.

Do these and you won't have any trouble with the Army.

For what happens when you don't do them, let us now look into the case of Private Hargrove, U.S.A.

This morning—our first morning in the Recruit Reception Center—began when we finished breakfast and started cleaning up our squadroom. A gray-haired, fatherly old private, who swore that he had been demoted from master sergeant four times, lined us up in front of the barracks and took us to the dispensary.

If the line in front of the mess hall dwindled as rapidly as the one at the dispensary, life would have loveliness to sell above its private consumption stock. First you're fifteen feet from the door, then (whiff) you're inside. Then you're standing between two orderlies and the show is on.

The one on my left scratched my arm and applied the smallpox virus. The only thing that kept me from keeling over was the hypodermic needle loaded with typhoid germs, which propped up my right arm.

From the dispensary we went to a huge warehouse of a building by the railroad tracks. The place looked like Goldenberg's Basement on a busy day. A score of fitters measured necks, waists, inseams, heads, and feet.

My shoe size, the clerk yelled down the line, was ten and a half.

"I beg your pardon," I prompted, "I wear a size nine."

"Forgive me," he said, a trifle weary, "the expression is 'I wore a size nine.' These shoes are to walk in, not to make you look like Cinderella. You say size nine; your foot says ten and a half."

We filed down a long counter, picking up our allotted khaki and denims, barrack bags and raincoats, mess kits and tent halves. Then we were led into a large room, where we laid aside the vestments of civil life and donned our new garments.

While I stood there, wondering what I was supposed to do next, an attendant caught me from the rear and strapped to my shoulders what felt like the Old Man of the Mountain after forty days.

"Straighten up, soldier," the attendant said, "and git off the floor. That's nothing but a full field pack, such as you will tote many miles before you leave this man's Army. Now I want you to walk over to that ramp and over it. That's just to see if your shoes are comfortable."

I looked across the room to where an almost perpendicular walkway led up to and over a narrow platform.

"With these Oregon boots and this burden of misery," I told him firmly, "I couldn't even walk over to the thing. As for climbing over it, not even an alpenstock, a burro train, and two St. Bernard dogs complete with brandy could get me over it."

There was something in his quiet, steady answering glance that reassured me. I went over the ramp in short order. On the double, I think the Army calls it.

From there we went to the theater, where we were given intelligence tests, and to the classification office, where we were interviewed by patient and considerate corporals.

"And what did you do in civil life?" my corporal asked me.

"I was feature editor of the Charlotte News."

"And just what sort of work did you do, Private Hargrove? Just give me a brief idea."

Seven minutes later, I had finished answering the question.

"Let's just put down here, 'Editorial worker.' " He sighed compassionately. "And what did you do before all that?"

I told him. I brought in the publicity work, the soda-jerking, the theater ushering, and the printer's deviling.

"Private Hargrove," he said, "the Army is just what you have needed to ease the burdens of your existence. Look no farther, Private Hargrove, you have found a home."

The word "buddy" hadn't come into popularity yet in the new Army. I suppose that if there were such things, Maury Sher would be mine. Sher and I occupied adjoining bunks when I was in Battery A. I bummed most of my cigarettes from him and we always got into trouble together.

Private Sher is a smart and likable Jewish boy from Columbus, Ohio. He went to school at Southern California, until he learned that all the world's knowledge doesn't come from the intellectual invalids who usually teach the 8:30 class. Then he went back to Columbus, had an idea patented, and built himself a restaurant shaped like a champagne glass.

Came the fateful Sixteenth of October and Sher enrolled for the Selective Service System. His application was accepted last July and, since he had been the successful proprietor of a restaurant, he was classified as a promising student for the Army cooking course.

The two of us got together when he was sent to the Replacement Center here. We started an acquaintance when I topped all his Jewish jokes and began teaching him how to speak Yiddish. I was attracted by his native intelligence, his pleasant personality, his sense of humor, the similarity of his likes and dislikes to mine, his subscription to *PM*, his well-stocked supply of cigarettes (my brand), and the cookies he constantly received from home.

So we became more or less constant companions. We made the rounds here together, went to Charlotte together, made goo-goo eyes at the same waitress in Fayetteville, and swapped valuable trade secrets in goldbricking [shirking assigned work].

There was one Sunday evening when Sher started a letter to his family and found, after a couple of paragraphs, that there was nothing for him to write about. "Here, Junior," he said. "Write a letter for your old daddy. Give them the old Hargrovian schmaltz."

Since Junior was in a devilish mood, he sat down and wrote a long and inspired letter to the Shers of Columbus, Ohio—telling them how their little Maurice was falling behind in his classes by goldbricking and hanging out late at the Service Club, entreating them to return him to his true career, the Army. I finished by saying, "You see who's writing the letters; you should know where to send the cookies. Forget that bum Maury."

Several days later—after I had swapped my skillet for a typewriter and had moved to Headquarters Battery—I came by Battery A to see if I had any mail from my nonwriting friends in Charlotte. There weren't any letters, but there was a package which looked about the size of a steamer trunk. There were enough cookies inside to feed a small regiment for three days.

The card inside read: "Dear Hargrove—We think your idea about the cookies is superb. Give Maury one or two; he's a good boy when he wants to be. Why don't you come up to Columbus on your furlough?"

It seemed that this beautiful friendship—with all its fragrant memories, its happy hours of hell-raising, its beautiful cigarettes, cookies, and Samaritan relatives—was destined to end with the closing of the basic training cycle here.

I had already left Battery A for another residential section a half-mile away. We managed to get together three or four times a week for a movie, a trip to Fayetteville, or a pleasant evening of bull-shooting at the Service Club. But even this was to pass.

Sher's own thirteen weeks were drawing to a close and he was slated to be assigned to a permanent station as a cook. With sinking hearts, we watched group after group leave for camps in Louisiana, Georgia, Missouri, New York, Michigan.

And then pleasant news came over the grapevine telegraph. Private Maurice Sher, by reason of skill, application, and neatness, had been assigned as a cook for the Center Headquarters officers' mess.

It's only latrine gossip, but if it comes through it means that Private Sher will be transferred to Headquarters Battery and the team of Hargrove and Sher will ride again.

---

★

---

From *The GI War, 1941–1945*, by Ralph G. Martin (Avon, 1967)

## THE SERGEANT
by Private Joe Sims

I do not like the sergeant's face,
I do not like his chatter.
And what I think about his brain
Is censorable matter.

He sits in a tent
At the end of the street
And clutters the desk
With his oversized feet.

I do not like the sergeant's nose.
It would look better broken.
I do not like his tone of voice
When drill-commands are spoken.

He walks in the rear
When we're out on march,
And never relaxes
To "Route step Harch!"

I do not like the sergeant's views
On Army life and such,
But what I think about the sarge
Don't seem to matter much.

He can still pull his rank
When I enter my pleas
And when I find myself stuck
With the chronic KPs.

---

★

---

From *More G.I. Laughs: Real Army Humor*, selected by Harold Hersey
(Sheridan House, 1944)

## THE LOWLY ROOKIE
by Jefferson Barracks Hub

Under a spreading shelter half
　　A lowly rookie lies;
The rook a sorry lad is he,
　　With aching arms and thighs;
And the muscles of his aching back,
　　Bring only tears and sighs.

His hair was sleek and black and long,
   They called him "Dapper Dan."
Now his brow is wet with honest sweat,
   And he rests where e'er he can,
And looks each non-com in the face,
   For he loathes them to a man.

For thirteen weeks from morn' til night,
   You can see his muscles grow;
As you watch him calesthenic
   In cadence fast and slow;
Like a puppet on a bright red string
   In a hurdy-gurdy show.

If he forgets to comb his hair,
   He's gigged upon the spot;
They love to give a choice detail
   For a wrinkle in his cot,
Which only proves to each of them
   That what it takes, he's got.

Toiling-Rejoicing-Sorrowing,
   Onward through "basic" he goes;
Each morning sees him "falling out"
   Fatigued from head to toes.
Everything attempted, something done,
   He'll earn a night's repose.

————————————————————— ★ —————————————————————

From *Gone With the Draft: Love Letters of a Trainee*, by Park Kendall (M. S. Mill Co., Inc., 1941). Misspellings are as in the original.

Camp Orkway USA
Thursday

Deare Annie,

Well, Annie, I guess you will be surprised to learn that I am still in the service in an Uncle sams training camp. Yesir, I am still staying with it. I am kind of an old timer now. Today makes the sixth day in the army, Annie. It doesn't seem possible. I can do the rest of them without even counting. I should be back home in 359 days, Annie. I will bounce through this selective service training like a jitbugger at a dance. Patreeotic. That theres me, Annie. As along as Im stuck for it.

Ive changed a lot since I saw you though. I got on army underwear now, Annie. They issued me a uniform which I got on to. I wish you could see me. It fits good. That is it fits good where it touches. They give me a four piece outfit including two leggens. The laces fit fine in the leggens. I knowd I looked pretty snappy sos I asked the cook if he didn't think I got a good fit. He says it looked more like a stroke to him. He was just kidding. On facts as it were, Annie. I wished you could see me. The only defects is that the blouse is a little short but the pants fit good around the shoulders. I wished you could see me as you will have to start getting used to it and it will take time. Its kinda hard to get credit for standing at attention because my uniform is allways at ease. That's army expressions I picked up here,

Annie. The supply sargeant was allright though and tried to get us fitted correctly. He asked me if I preferred my uniform too big or too small. I thought he was kidding until I tried it on, but they dont kid much in the army on duty, Annie. The army sargeants are strict and businesslike but you can tell he had a sense of humor when you see me in my uniform.

I hope you will remember to thin of me once in a while, Annie, because we was friends to long. We might even have got married to each other, eh Annie, who knows? It wouldnt help any now because the allready got me ina camp. Perhaps when this emergency is over we can go around together some more. If you still want to I mean and are working. Anyway, I want you to know that I will allways remember you as the girl I got in the emergency, Annie.

I missed you a lot untill they sent us down to the stables. We were detailed to get some straw for bed ticks instead of matresses. I dont think it will catch on with the public, though, Annie. Its too lumpy. You can sleep on it if you have to though. Its a matter of midn over mattress. Straw is allright for horses bedding or elephants or cows or your fat Aunt Emma. Remember me kindly to her, Annie. Also give my best regards to your Uncle Eb. By the way, Annie, a fellow up here that knows your Uncle Eb says he aint enrolled at that school what learns you how to become a bartender. Your Uncle Eb goes there but he aint studying nothing. He just hangs around to drink the mistakes. I guess you cant help it if you are punchy at times with such a family. Remember me kindly to your mother, Annie.

We got a swell leader. His name is Captain Abbott. A new recruit says it was Capsule Abbott instead of Captain. I knowed better. I told him it was a capsule what got us in the army but it is a Captain that is keeping us in. Aint it the truth, Annie, aint it the truth?

We all got military titles up here like Major or General. I made up my mind I would accept anything they wanted to give me. So for a title they gave me Private Hicks. Dont ask me why, Annie, because nothing is private. They even open my postcards and tell me that my mother is sending my overshoes with a fruitcake and that grandpa got ahold of some cooking brandy and tried to bring a horse in the kitchen.

That was a swell party you gave at your house, Annie, to show how much you appreciated me going away for a year. Everything was fine except I will not beat around the bush about that fellow with the little mustache which you invited. You hurt me then, Annie. Him and me was lifting a couple in the kitchen. He says he hoped the draft board would see his dependents in the right light. I didn't know he had any dependents but he says sure he has. He says they are the Wilkins family. You better watch out, Annie, you might get mixed up with moonshiners.

When you write be sure and put some of these on your letter X X x x You savvy, Annie? Ha ha

Yours faithfully untill I get out,
Joe

PS Address letters or packages which we are encouraged to receive to Private Joe Hicks which will reach em that way in the army. Some fellows have got pies but I would rather you suggested it. Remember me kindly to your mother if she cooks anything.

*Some months later:*

Camp Orkway U S A
Tuesday

Deare Annie,

    We been getting instructions in first aid. Thats what to do before it is to late and the doctor arrives. It learns you to tell how a person is feeling by observing there symptoms. For instance when your Uncle Eb is intoxicated his symptoms would be unsteadiness and your Aunt Emmas symptoms would be glaring of the eyeballs, bursting of the blood vessels, and falling of the arches. They also gave us lectures on sanitation and personal hygiene and how to avoid germs. One of the old soldiers up here says we ought to sign a non-aggression pact with the cooties right away. He says its going to be fierce now that they have got the right to organize and participate in collective bargaining.

    We had a practice black out march the other night. Thats to see how far you can march in the dark without lighting a cigarette. We was advancing under the cover of darkness to surprise an imaginary enemy. We went up back roads and surprised a lot of cows. A farmer came out on his porch with a gun and a lantern. I guess he thought we were after his chickens. He didn't start anything when he seen we had him outnumbered. We wore rain coats because there was an imaginary rain. I told the sargeant if they had let me know a couple of days ahead of time I would have shined my shoes and had my suit pressed. That always brings on a rain. We marched about twenty miles and slept in an armory on imaginary beds.

Part of the way we wore our gas masks to get used to them. I lifted mine to get a little fresh air, but we were going past a hog ranch at the time. When I got a sniff I could tell it wasnt imaginary hogs. I could tell they were real from there body odor. I guess pigs never studied personal hygiene.

The next day we marched back in daylight down the highway. I wanted to thumb a ride but the sargant says it was good for me to have "a little sun and air." Just for fun I says Gosh sargant, that would be embarrassing. I aint even married. He never said nothing. He seen I had him. Always clowning, eh Annie.

One of the fellows says he seen a buzzard. I says Lets dont talk that way about the sargant. We passed a lot of cows in a field. I says to Bill Ashbury that they was awful fat. He says Yes they was. On this side anyway. When we got back to camp the Major gave us a talk. He says we done swell. That is all but us fellows in Company B. He says I want to compliment you sons of Company A on your splendid showing. But I cant say as much for you sons of B.

We sure slept when we got to bed that night. Buddy Post says he wont ever walk in his sleep again. He used to sit around in an office all day. He says he used to walk in his sleep sos he would get his rest and exercise at the same time. While we was on the hike we passed a couple of Nudist camps which are located around here. A Nudist camp is just like a summer resort with a wonderful view of everything. Once in a while some of them come into town but they wear clothes in the main business section.

Yours truly,
Joe

It was morning roll call at Fort Dix. The sergeant called out, "Platoon, atten-HUT! Private Michaels, report to the main office. Your brother died last night."

The chaplain could only look on in horror. Afterwards, he approached the sergeant. "That is a cruel and unfeeling way to break tragic news to someone. We must be much more gentle and less abrupt in the future."

The sergeant shrugged. "Yes sir. I'll try to remember that."

Several days later, a call came in about another soldier's loss.

As the troops assembled for morning roll call, the chaplain stepped forward. "Let me handle this one, Sergeant," he said. He turned toward the sleepy soldiers and said, "Platoon, atten-HUT !"

They came to attention.

"Good morning, men!" the chaplain said.

"Good morning, sir," they replied.

"Men, today is Mother's Day, and I hope all of you will be calling home to send your moms a loving thought. In fact, all of you who are fortunate enough to still have a mother who's alive and well, take two steps forward. Private Jones— not so fast!"

★

From *Artie Greengroin, Pfc.*, by Harry Brown (Knopf, 1945)

*Editor's Note*: Harry Brown left his editorial position at *The New Yorker* in 1941, when he entered the Army. When *Yank:*

*The Army Weekly* was organized in May 1942, Brown became its acting managing editor, and by the time he went to England early in 1943 to help out with the British edition of *Yank*, he was an associate editor. It was then that Brown created Artie Greengroin, whose adventures first delighted *Yank*'s readers.

Brown wrote in 1945: "Artie Greengroin was created in the grimly fabulous time when we were building up our military strength in Britain in preparation for the invasion of Europe. That time came abruptly to an end on June 6, 1944, and already it is growing misty and is being veiled in a glamour it certainly never deserved. It was a period in which the average American soldier, in a foreign country for many more months than he had ever thought possible, was alternately bored, astonished, delighted, and depressed by what he saw about him. In a time of enforced inactivity he chafed at the bit and groused. Out of the chafing and grousing came Artie Greengroin.

Through him it was possible to poke fun at the things the average soldier did not like—swagger sticks, campaign ribbons for non-existent campaigns, endless inspections, countless shots in the arm, eternal drilling of both the parade-ground and field sort, Army food. Most of the things he did not like were necessary things, but that did not stop him from complaining. Complaint was his ancient and inalienable right; Artie merely transferred that ancient and inalienable right to the printed page. And I think his character was appreciated by those who were living with someone like him and listening to him every day.

## The First of Artie

I first ran into Artie Greengroin at Fort Belvoir, Virginia. It was pure accident. The company was getting some training on crawling under barb wire; three non-coms were blind-folded and placed on the other side of a long double apron. We had to crawl under the wire in full field equipment, and if one of the blindfolded non-coms heard a man scrape against the wire and pointed at him, said man could con-sider himself machine-gunned for the rest of the exercise.

When my turn came, I lay flat and started to worm my way under the wire, digging my nose in the ground and slid-ing my rifle along beside me. I had wiggled about halfway through when something clanked against my bayonet. It was the helmet of another crawler and under the helmet was the pale, pinched, pasty face of Artie Greengroin.

The blindfolded non-coms set up a howl and we were waved from under the wire, presumably corpses. As we got to our feet Artie said his first words. "Them rummies got ears like bunny rabbits," he said.

I remarked that a deaf old man in a sound-proof room would have been able to hear that clank.

"Maybe," Artie said grudgingly. "When a man's ears is inured to the noises of New York a little clank is apt to pass unnoticed. Less go over unner a tree and have a fag."

We went over under a tree and had a fag. "Wass your name?" Artie wanted to know. "My name's Greengroin, ole Artie Greengroin. I use to drive a hoise around Berklyn."

I told him my name. "You used to drive a what?" I asked.

"A hoise," Artie said. "For carting stiffs."

"Oh," I said.

"But now I'm in the blassid old Armey," said Artie.

"So's practically everyone else in the country," I said.

"Ah, I know that," said Artie, "but when they take me they're trying to make a killer out of a fine, sensitive soul. I was made for better things than being a sodjer. Look, I been in this company two weeks and what have they loined me? They loined me how to put up a bridge. I don't want to put up no bridges. They loined me how to march in chorus. I don't want to do no marching in chorus or otherwise. There's no two ways about it, they got the wrong man in ole Artie."

"What will you do about it?" I asked.

"Make the most of it," Artie said. "Us Greengroins awways make the most of things. 'Stick with the woild,' is our motter. A man's got to sink or swim these days, gaw-dam it."

"Right you are," I said.

"I'm strikly a swimmer," said Artie.

"That's the way to be," I said.

"Nevertheless, I oney been here two weeks and awready I think of the olden days all the time," Artie said. "The trouble with me is I'm a borned civilian at heart. Still, I got to make the most of it. I ought to be a capting in a couple of months. I got poise. I got determination. I got sensitiveness. I got jess the qualities a leader needs. When I get to be a capting I'll put you in my company and treat you right."

"Thanks, Artie," I said.

"Don't mention it," said Artie. "I'm awways glad to help a friend in need. You know what they ought to have kicking around here? They ought to have a portable beer wagon."

"Why?" I asked.

Artie looked astonished. "Why?" he echoed. "Because you can get a drink of beer out of a portable beer wagon. A guy crawls around on his gut all morning, he gets thoisty. I been crawling around on my gut all morning. I'm thoisty. It's as simple as that."

"So it is," I said.

"Thass the trouble with this Army," Artie said. "It don't look out for its employees."

"A shameful oversight," I said.

"They's lots of little things they could do to make things inneresting," Artie said. "I got a lot of ideas on the subjeck. One of these days I'm going to pop in on a couple of coinels and show them wass wrong with the Armed Forces. Maybe they'll gimme a medal."

"Maybe not," I said.

"Probly not," said Artie. "Theys selfish ole bassars, them coinels. Keep yer buttons polished, they say. Clean yer gun. Thass no way to run a Army. You got to be polite to get any-wheres with people. Now, look at them guys crawling under the barb wire. Are they happy? Naw, they ain't happy. And the reason they ain't happy is because they got a slew of blas-sid sergeants standing over them making them get down on their gut. If them sergeants should say: 'Please, mister, get down on your gut and crawl unner the barb wire,' they'd be glad to oblige for the good of the country. Thass the way I look at things!"

"Very sound," I said.

"Now, I'm a man that's had a very inneresting oily life," Artie said. "I'm full of experience tempered by poise. I'm going to get a long ways in the Army before I get done with it. All I'm doing now is setting around, fining out how the joint works. As soon as I fine out, I'll start to rise up the rungs of the ladder."

"Hey, Greengroin," someone shouted. It was one of the sergeants—evidently Artie's sergeant.

"Don't pay no attention to him," Artie said. "He's awways wanting me for menial tasks. I ignore him, the rummy."

"You think that's a good idea?" I asked.

"Everything's a good idea that woiks," Artie said.

"Does ignoring the sergeant work?" I wanted to know.

"As a matter of fack, it don't," Artie said. "But I'm getting on to him. I'll have him eating goobers out of me mitt before very long."

The sergeant came up to where we were standing. "I been calling you, Greengroin," he said.

"Was you, sergeant?" Artie asked innocently. "I was stanning here with a butt in me mouth and I didn't hear nothing."

"Can you hear me now?" asked the sergeant.

"Yerse, sergeant," Artie said.

The sergeant smiled grimly. "Well, Greengroin," he said, "one of the KP's was tooken sick and I suddenly remembered you was a fass man with a cup and saucer, so I got you the job of taking his place. Yer hired, Greengroin."

"I was on KP yesterday, sergeant," Artie said.

"Yer broke in, then," said the sergeant. "You knows yer job. Gwan down and see the cook before I beat your brains out." With this the sergeant took his charming self off.

"Thass the way it is, every day," Artie said wearily. "That sergeant don't like me because I took six bucks off him in a craps game. A vile character, that sergeant."

"You'd better go down and see the cook," I said.

"Yerse, I better," Artie said. "As long as I don't see the mess sergeant."

"What's the matter with the mess sergeant?" I asked.

"I took eight bucks offf him in a craps game," Artie said. "He hates me woist of all. Soreheaded ole bassars, ain't they?"

And with that he wandered off to find the cook. As I watched him go I decided that he was the only grown-up Dead End Kid I had ever seen. I ran into him occasionally at Fort Belvoir, but I really got to know him only after we were shipped to England.

# SHIPPING OUT:
# READY OR NOT

From *c/o Postmaster*, by Corporal Thomas R. St. George (Thomas Y. Crowell Co., 1943)

One bright morning, early in the spring of 1942, fifty-seven average young men were rousted out of a West Coast barracks at the brutal hour of 5 a.m., pushed into the semblance of a straight line, and informed by a captain (who played to the hilt this reasonable facsimile of a "zero hour") that they were on shipment. At least six of the fifty-seven received this news with practically no feeling whatsoever, having spent the night wallowing in what passed for vice in Paso Robles, California. Particularly one of them, a married man himself, had talked with a waitress for all of ten minutes, or until she'd repeated several times that she was married herself, to a sergeant in Fort Lewis. The others had sat around and gloried in such wallowing, smoked too much, drank too many alleged whiskey-cokes, and come home by special request of the Provost Marshal.

Now, at 5 a.m., they were in no way as bright as the morning. But such is the power of the G.I. mind that before breakfast was over all were firmly convinced they would arrive at Fort Leonard Wood in time for a weekend pass, and two had laid exhaustive plans as to what they would do first chance they got home to Des Moines. All of which resulted from a chance remark, dropped by a lieutenant colonel and overheard by a KP, to the effect that men on shipment would be leaving the Ninth Corps Area.

Well, great! We were leaving the Ninth Corps Area! Back to the Middle West. It was with reasonably light hearts that we packed our barracks bags. (Reasonably light hearts and shoes and socks and three kinds of underwear and a carton of cigarettes and a cherished garrison cap and a sheaf of old letters.) Whistled outside for the last time at eight-thirty, we were lined up in a double row and minutely inspected for scuffed shoes and unbuttoned buttons. No commander in his right mind would think of turning a soldier over to another commander without said soldier's looking ten degrees snappier than an enlistment poster. Soldiers with flat feet, yes; soldiers with a rifle score of 35, yes; confirmed goldbricks and cigarette moochers, take 'em and you're welcome, sir; but sloppy soldiers, never!

Buttoned to the ears and standing at attention, we listened to a short lecture (prepared by the War Department and butchered by a second lieutenant) to the effect that we were undoubtedly the finest type of Young Americans, leaving to defend our heritage. We thought of the advantages of defending a heritage in Fort Leonard Wood as compared with San Luis Obispo and were considerably happier than our lieutenant throughout the performance. Our company commander, who had been with us something under two weeks, then bid us goodbye and good luck and added that we were potentially the finest soldiers he had ever seen. We were deeply impressed.

Staff Sergeant Beerbodt, recently promoted on the strength of our improved appearance after thirteen weeks of his guidance, led us as we straggled across the parade ground. Not once did he shout, "Cover off! Soldier up!" Now it is naturally impossible to march decently with two barracks bags taking turns at knocking the legs from under one and Sergeant Beerbodt knew this as well as we did; but thirteen weeks before, when we were raw recruits, Sergeant Beerbodt had led us across this same parade ground and that night he had barked at us constantly, "Pick it up! Pick it up! Stay in line!" As of then, we hated Sergeant Beerbodt passionately. During thirteen weeks of listening to Sergeant Beerbodt shout, "Right shoulder . . . HARMS! Forward . . . HARCH! C'mon, c'mon, DO it!," our hatred increased until at times it threatened to choke us.

But now, as we straggled across our parade ground for the last time, Sergeant Beerbodt was suddenly a friend. At least his ugly face was familiar and only the night before he had confided to three of us (over a beer that we had purchased, which may have had something to do with it) that we were, "Aw'right guys only you louse around too much." And he'd given us a bit of advice: "Just keep your nose clean an' don't get caught lousin' around an' you will be okay." We'd learned a lot of things from Sergeant Beerbodt besides the Manual of Arms. So now, as we waited at the edge of the parade ground for nobody knew just what, we offered him a cigarette. And he—it was the first time in our experience—countered with one of his own.

More soldiers arrived as we waited, straggling across the parade ground from all directions, and all, we discovered, quite sure that they were going to Alaska or Los Angeles or Texas or the Portland Air Base. We held ourselves somewhat aloof; obviously we were going to Fort Leonard Wood for a reason. To form the nucleus of a new division, it was decided, and presently there was a spirited discussion as to how much money a tech sergeant made. We would all be tech sergeants immediately, of course, with a new division.

Eventually there were olive drab overcoats and blue barracks bags scattered along five hundred yards of parade ground. Half a dozen officers remained apart, bearing the weight of the war on their shoulders, while we enlisted men sat around and talked of girls and home and various towns in the vicinity of various camps. Next to me two lawyers discussed at length the divorce laws of the State of Washington. Most of us, I think, in spite of what we had offered at times during the past weeks if only we could "get outta this HOLE," were really sorry to be going. Leaving a home is always sad, and a soldier has so many homes.

And the Army has an antidote. After two hours spent sitting on a barracks bag (which invariably has a pair of shoes, heels up, directly beneath the back of a guy's lap when he sits down) or the granulated surface of a parade ground, anything, even an Army truck, looks like a change for the better. At long last such trucks arrived, and after a considerable amount of lining up and counting off, we were ordered into them. Those of us who fancied we were going east had somehow imagined we would travel in the comparative comfort of a troop train, but having had nothing to do with planning our itinerary (and because it was an order) we took the trucks.

In fact, we made a concerted rush for them, proving once and for all that we were veterans by everybody's trying to get in first and sit at the back where he could at least see where he'd been if not where he was going. After a certain amount of waiting and the addition, under protest, of three more soldiers complete with barracks bags, we pulled out. Civilian traffic being blocked off, we roared through the Main Gate without slackening speed. We derived a strange pleasure from this. It was the only time any of us had ever come through that gate without showing a pass to the M.P.

An Army truck as a means of transportation may be excellent for shipping cabbage or livestock, but as rubberneck bus it is a fizzle. All I saw as we roared north was the back of the guy's neck that sat on my lap, a peculiarly uninspiring view. And a convoy, when seen from the rear seat of a passing sedan, may look very impressive and may even fill the sedan's occupants with a fleeting pride in the "power and the might of the American Army"; but like a parade, it is best appreciated from the sidelines. The steel-helmeted troops sitting grimly in the backs of the trucks are probably impressed not at all with the "power and the might." They are chiefly interested in finding a speck of what passes for comfort while en route; they wait hopefully while some hardy soul lights a cigarette and promptly bum him for a light; they'd like to know who the hell is trying to sprawl in a truck full of twenty-two men; and they wonder vaguely how long it will be before their driver hooks the corner of a concrete spillway and jars everybody loose from his heredity. That he will hit one sooner or later they know.

Thus we roared north. Three times we stopped so that a lieutenant might stick his head over the endgate and count us. This counting is an important part of all troop movements, there being a not-unfounded belief that in any given number of soldiers being moved from one place to another, ten percent will, without even trying, become "lost" unless closely watched and carefully counted. The fact that our truck was accused at various times of containing 23, 19, and 18 men has nothing to do with it. Nor can the fact that on arrival two trucks were discovered missing be considered as proof of anything. Quite possibly somebody forgot to count the trucks. All of which is the kind of thing soldiers mean when they say "the old Army game."

Anyway, we arrived. Exactly where was questionable, but we detrucked in one of those slow, penetrating drizzles California reserves for soldiers who insist they would rather be back home in Sioux City. We attempted to reclaim our barracks bags as they were hurled out of the trucks by soldiers doing their best to resemble old and calloused baggage handlers. Then we waited. Various non-coms wandered about wondering audibly as to who we were and where did we belong? One of us who fancied himself a man of the world asked a corporal, "How long you been in, pal?"

"Twenty-two months," the corporal told him.

We subsided. These men were veterans.

Eventually an officer arrived and herded us into a barracks. He was visibly worried to find that we had arrived with nothing in the way of equipment outside of gas masks and went off muttering that we were supposed to arrive with everything *except* gas masks. He was replaced, presently, by a first lieutenant, who herded us into a mess hall, and, when we were done eating, led us back to the barracks, told us to stay there. His duty done, he promptly disappeared. He, in turn, was replaced by a first sergeant who informed us we were temporarily assigned to "Hache" co. ("It says 'G' on the buildings, but it's Hache!"), and mustn't go away because somebody might want us. He seemed extremely doubtful as to whether or not anybody would actually want us, and was on the point of disappearing himself but stopped at the door, and in the manner of a great man dispensing small favors told us, "You can take off them ties now. We don't wear 'em here."

Religiously we removed our ties. And gathered in little groups the forty-one of us who were left (the remaining sixteen, as far as I know, are still roaring north in the back of an Army truck and should be well along on the Alaskan Highway by this time) decided—not without misgiving—that "we just came in out of the rain."

As it turned out, this idea was somewhat erroneous. The next time any of us mentioned it we were six hundred miles off the coast of Hawaii. By that time we had become more or less resigned to the series of jolts that transformed us, in something less than a week, from the Basic Training or "Glorified Boy Scout" stage of soldiering to the ranks of rough, tough, case-hardened, blasé Combat Troops en route to a Theater of Operations. In a word: no, we did not go to Fort Leonard Wood.

Considerable doubt as to the exact whereabouts of our destination crept in while we were still temporarily assigned to "Hache" co. By dint of persistent questioning we discovered that "Sure, this outfit has trucks, but they's all at the Point of Embarkation!" We learned too that the remainder of the company or "old men" were entirely National Guardsmen or low-numbered selectees with eighteen months of service including the Louisiana Maneuvers behind them. We "new men," who still figured our service in weeks, felt out of our depth. Then, late the second afternoon, we were herded into the supply room and issued new "coal scuttle" helmets. These, while undeniably a safer hat than our former "Dache" models, were still scarce enough in the spring of '42 to make us wonder just why *we* should be so honored. Unless, of course, we were ... But no! They couldn't send us! We weren't *ready*!

Ready or not we spent the following a.m. listening to a lecture on "Shipboard Discipline" and some off-the-record but highly colorful account of the Louisiana Maneuvers as seen by an enlisted man who began them as a sergeant and finished them digging latrines. In the afternoon we "new men" were given a physical examination and an interview. The former consisted of perfunctory tappings and the question: "Is anything wrong with you?" The accepted answer being (except in the case of a young man who had lost part of his plate in transit and was therefore quite helpless when confronted with G.I. food) "No, Sir." The interview, too, like a Post Exchange haircut, was short and quick. "What did you do in civilian life?" they asked us; "Next man!" Did the interviewing officer suspect a gleam of intelligence or discover a potential company barber, he took the man's name.

Immediately following our physical and interview, we were permanently assigned in alphabetical order, which might lead one to believe that our various abilities were not too carefully weighed. But, as one company commander explained to a bunch of the boys who showed up in a rifle platoon protesting that they were "communications men," what the Army really wanted was qualified killers, one to a gun. This little speech went a long way toward reviving the battered spirits of the misplaced communications men. It restored to them the feeling that they were important and led them to appear noticeably murderous for several weeks. Eleven of us, from Reem, Robert, to Terrell, Opaz, plus a strange youth who arrived via typographical error and was questioned at length concerning how the hell you pronounced "R-f-f-e-l-d-t," found ourselves intact and assigned to a headquarters company. Where we listened to a short succinct speech by the C.O., the gist of which was: "You men are going on a trip, by boat, and what you don't need, get rid of!" Ready or not, we were going.

Generally speaking, there was a mad rush to write, wire, and phone home, collect. And there were sundry blanks to fill in and forms to fill out, including a postcard signed by us and addressed to our "Next of Kin" but mailed (we sincerely hoped) sometime in the future by an official source, that conveyed the most banal but welcome message I ever hope to send anybody: "Arrived safely at destination." Incidentally, the words "next of kin" appeared on all these blanks with what seemed to me a thoroughly discouraging and unnecessary prominence.

Then there was a considerable amount of packing and repacking to be done. That which we thought we would need or could use while aboard ship we put in a barracks bag marked "A bag"; said bag to be our constant companion for the duration of the voyage. That which we decided we could neither need nor use until after "arriving safely at destination," we put in a "*B* bag," this one to travel on its own with no guarantee that we would ever see it again. On finishing my first packing I found this *B* bag contained one tool, for entrenching. Two strong men could scarcely lift my *A* bag. On the off chance that we would "arrive safely" in Australia, which was reputedly hot and dry, I added overshoes and two blankets and some odd garments affectionately known as "long johns" to the *B* bag (had we "arrived safely" in Alaska I would have suffered horribly) and eventually, after repeated efforts and a brutal slashing of nonessential goods, I got my *A* bag down to a mere eighty pounds.

Finally there was one last pass. Four of us took it together, spending a rather delightful Sunday afternoon— our "last in the good old U.S.A.," as we frequently reminded each other—in Monterey, a town that we had never seen before, will probably never see again, and did not see very much of that afternoon. Having a total of something like two dollars (borrowed) myself, I thought the prevailing spirit of "one for all and all for one" suited me admirably. And the fact that we were possessed of vital strategic knowledge—knowledge of supreme importance to the war effort— not to be bandied lightly about with the casual young lady acquaintances who became attached to us for rations and quarters in one of the bars, but only hinted at—more broadly as the day wore on—added greatly to our enjoyment. Frankly, the young ladies were impressed not at all with our guarded remarks concerning this imminent departure to fight, as one of us put it, "for *their* homes and *their* unborn children." Probably they'd heard substantially the same story from innumerable Presidio inductees on their way to Camp Haan.

Somewhat later, when not one of us could dance and two of us showed signs of becoming violently ill, the young ladies left. We took a taxi back to camp. At least we'd gone out in the approved fashion.

So long, town.

★

From *The Best from* Yank, *the Army Weekly* (Dutton, 1945)

## FIRST EPISTLE TO THE SELECTEES
according to Private First Class Harold Fleming

Lo, all ye miserable sinners, entering through the Gate of Induction *into* the land of Khaki, hearken unto my words; for I *have* dwelt in this land for many months and mine eyes have witnessed all manner of folly and *woe*.

2  Verily have I tasted of the bitter Fruit of TS *and* drained the dregs of the Cup of Snafu:

3  Gird up thy loins, my son, and take *up* the olive drab; but act slowly and with exceeding care and hearken first to the counsel of a wiser and sadder man than thou:

4  Beware thou the Sergeant *who* is called First; he hath a pleased and foolish look but he concealeth a serpent in his heart.

5  Avoid *him* when he speaketh low and his lips smileth; he smileth not for thee; his heart rejoiceth at *the* sight of thy youth and thine ignorance.

6   He will smile and smile and work all manner of evil against thee. A wise man shuns the orderly room, but the fool *shall* dwell in the kitchen forever.

7   Unto all things there is a time: there is a time to speak and a time to be silent: be thou like unto stone in the *presence* of thy superiors, and keep thy tongue still when they shall call for volunteers.

8   The wise man searcheth out the easy details, but only a fool sticketh out *his* neck.

9   Look thou with disfavor upon the newly made corporal; he prizeth *much* his stripes and is proud and foolish; he laugheth and joketh much with the older noncoms and looketh *upon* the private with a frown.

10  He would fain go to OCS, but he is not qualified.

11  Know thou that the Sergeant of the Mess is a man of many moods: when *he* looketh pleased and his words are like honey, the wise KP seeketh him out and praiseth his chow and laugheth much at his jests:

12  But when he moveth with great haste and the sweat standeth *on* his brow *and* he *curseth* under his breath, make thyself scarce; for he will fall like a whirlwind upon the idle and the goldbrick shall know his wrath.

13  The Supply Sergeant is a lazy man *and* worketh not; but he is the keeper of many good things: if thou wouldst wear well-fitting raiment and avoid the statement of charges, *make* him thy friend.

14  He prizeth drunkenness *above* all things.

15  He careth not for praise or flattery, but lend him *thy* lucre and thy liquor and he will love thee.

16  Hell hath no fury like a Shavetail scored: he walketh with a swagger and regardeth the enlisted man with a

raised eyebrow; he looketh upon his bars with exceeding pleasure *and* loveth a salute mightily.

17 Act thou lowly unto him and call him sir and he will love thee.

18 Damned *be* he who standeth first in the line of chow and shortstoppeth the dessert and cincheth the coffee.

19 He taketh from the meat dish with a heavy hand and leaveth thee the bony *part*.

20 He is thrice cursed, and all *people*, even unto the pfcs, will revile him and spit upon him: *for* his name is called Chow Hound, and he is an abomination.

21 Know thou the Big Operator, but trust him *not*: he *worketh* always upon a deal and he speaketh confidentially.

22 He knoweth many women and goeth into town every night; he borroweth all thy money; yea, even *unto* thy ration check.

23 He promiseth to fix thee up, but doth *it* not.

24 Beware thou the Old Man, for he will make *thee* sweat; when he approacheth, look thou on the ball; he loveth to chew upon thy posterior.

25 Keep thou out of his sight and let him not *know* thee by name: for he who arouseth the wrath of the Old Man shall *go* many times unto the chaplain. *Selah*.

# IN THE FIELD, SEAS, AND SKIES

The company commander and the first sergeant were in the field for maneuvers. As they hit the sack for the night, the first sergeant said: "Sir, look up into the sky and tell me what you see."

"I see millions of stars," the commander replied.

The first sergeant asked, "What does that tell you, sir?"

The commander answered, "Astronomically, it tells me that there are millions of galaxies and potentially billions of planets. Theologically, it tells me that God is great and that we are small and insignificant. Meteorologically, it tells me that we will have a beautiful day tomorrow. What does it tell you, Top?"

The first sergeant said, "Well sir, it tells me that somebody stole our tent."

---

★

---

During training exercises, a lieutenant driving through the pouring rain along a muddy back road encountered another car seriously stuck in the mud on the roadside. "Your jeep stuck, sir?" the lieutenant asked the red-faced colonel as he pulled up alongside.

"Nope," replied the colonel, who emerged from the vehicle and handed the lieutenant the keys. "*Yours* is."

---

★

---

A new ensign was assigned to submarines, where he'd dreamed of working since the time he was a young boy. He was anxious to impress the master chief with his expertise learned studying subs carefully over the years, and he began prattling off all sorts of facts and figures.

The master chief cut him off quickly and said, "Listen, 'sir,' it's real simple. Add the number of times we dive to the number of times we surface. Divide that number by two. If the result doesn't come out even, don't open the hatch."

---

★

---

From *The GI War, 1941–1945*, by Ralph G. Martin (Avon, 1967)

Six [American] soldiers were luxuriating in a homemade shower unit right of the side of a road [in North Africa] when nurses from a nearby evacuation hospital tramped by. The soldiers were so surprised at seeing American women that they just stood out near the road and waved and yelled and whistled, completely forgetting that they were stark naked. The nurses just smiled, waved back, kept walking.

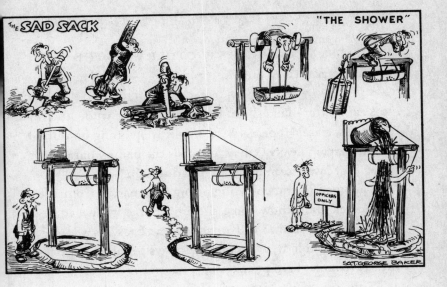

***

A lieutenant fresh from jumping instructions was seated next to a sergeant in a parachute regiment during a night-time exercise. The lieutenant looked very pale and frightened, so the sergeant struck up a conversation.

"Scared, Lieutenant?" he asked.

"No, just a bit apprehensive," the lieutenant replied.

"What's the difference?"

"Apprehensive means I'm scared with a college education."

***

From *The Best from* Yank, *the Army Weekly* (Dutton, 1945)

## HOPELESS MCGONIGLE'S BROTHER WINS THE DSC
by Staff Sergeant L. A. Brodsky

It is right after mail call, and me, Stripeless Murphy, and my main associate, Hopeless McGonigle, is reclining on our GI Beautyrests in Leaky Gables, which is the name what we give our home away from home for the duration.

I am just finishing reading a long explanation from a certain chick about how come she ain't home when I make a LD station-to-station call what sets me back a sawbuck to talk to her old lady, when Hopeless says to me, "Stripeless," he says to me, "I am puzzled."

This is a normal state of affairs, so I says, "What causes your puzzlement?"

"My brother," says Hopeless.

"I don't even know you got a brother," says I.

"He is formerly in the Army," says hopeless, "and he is now out."

"Why?" says I.

"I don't know," says Hopeless, "but in this letter he says something about street cleaning which he is getting for a reward."

"What you mean?" queries I.

"He got a DSC, what anybody knows stands for department of street cleaning."

"You," says I, "are a dope. Let me see the letter."

This is what I read:

"Dear Bro. Hopeless," the letter starts out. "It is a long

time since I am having the opportunity to write to you a letter, because as you know, I am with a Infantry outfit on a certain island where we are very busy swatting mosquitoes and little guys what eight out of ten wear glasses and got buck teeth which we kick out. The reason I got time to write is because I am now under the care of a bunch of pill rollers which is having a swell time putting me together like I used to be. I am all broken up following a certain thing for which I get a DSC and maybe even a Purple Heart."

Hopeless says to me, "Hey, Stripeless, see what my brother says about a Purple Heart? I am worried as I am thinking that my old grandmother, may she rest in peace, is dying of a purple heart and also diabetes."

"You are," says I, "a jerk. Let me continue this letter." I read on.

"So Bro.," continues the letter, "I shall tell you how I am getting busted up to pieces almost. It is like this.

"Last Wednesday I am sitting on a rock gnawing on my iron rations, when the lieut. comes up and says, 'McGonigle, I got a very important mission for you to execute.' To make a long story short I am getting a job as a advanced scout on the lookout for the enemy.

"So, I goes off into the jungle and locates a hollow tree what I climb into. I ain't in the tree no minute and a half when I hear two guys talking in a language what sounds like Donald Duck with static.

"Aha, says I to me, this must be rats.

"I am correct.

"I peek out a knothole and I see two of these little guys talking and one of them finally goes away and the other climbs into the tree what I am inside of and he hangs from a branch and starts throwing lead in the immediate vicinity of the direction from what I am coming from.

"I don't like this situation on account of there is a couple of guys back in camp what owe me dough from last pay day and if they get themselves air conditioned by this son of Tojo I ain't never going to collect my investment, so One-and-One, says I to me, you gotta stop this guy from being a nuisance and perchance making null and void several just debts you got outstanding. OK, I answers me, and starts looking around.

"This tree what I am squirreled up in is very narrow and I ain't got no maneuverability with a gun, but the tree is empty all the way up to the branch on which the son of the rising sun is located on, so I crawls on up to the branch to investigate. When I get up there I find that I can reach out and touch the Nip on account of there is a hole in the tree.

"I start thinking. One-and-One, says I to me, what are the brass hats always talking about. Firepower, I answers me in a flash. OK, One-and-One, I replies, you gotta use firepower. So I pull out a box of matches and go to work.

"Start at the bottom and work up is a good motto, I think, so I give this guy a hotfoot. I insert a match in the guy's shoe and light it. There is no response and the match goes out.

"You gotta increase firepower, says I to me, so I inserts two matches and light them. There still ain't no reaction. If I don't see it with my own eyes I would believe that I am dealing with a corpse as there ain't no guy what is still living that never jumped to a One-and-One-Makes-Three hotfoot. This situation is making me very angry. My professional pride is hurt. So I do something which ain't strictly ethical, but I am figuring that all is fair in love and war.

"I remember that the brass hats is always talking about strategy and attacking from the rear, so I take the packet of matches and stick them in the Jap's back pocket and light it. A merry blaze on the spot of the Jap's anatomy where the back goes off into the legs is the result. It blazes brightly.

"*Banzai*, yells the Jap and jumps off the tree.

"When I get down to the ground the Jap is got a broken neck and is dead besides.

"Your Faithful Bro.

"One-and-One-Makes-Three

"P.S. When they hear about what I do to the Jap I get a DSC.

"P.S. Jr. The reason I am in the hospital is because I try to collect my just debts and the guys what owe me the money find out I am charging interest. The Lieut. thinks I get these wounds in battle."

I hand the letter to Hopeless. "Hopeless," says I, "a DSC is a medal and you should be proud of your brother."

"I am," says Hopeless, "except I am worried about that Purple Heart business on account of they put my uncle Joseph Aloysius McGonigle in the nut house when he said he had blue blood."

---

★

---

Contributed to *Reader's Digest*'s "Humor in Uniform" by Cindy Brown

During the Second World War, my father-in-law was stationed at the Army Air corps base in Prestwick, Scotland. President Franklin Roosevelt was to make a visit at any time, and coded messages were used to alert the air tower of such top-secret arrivals. One night the tower received the message: "Big Dogs Arriving 0600." The next morning, as the plane landed on the runway, the entire base awaited the President and his officials. The cargo door opened, the band commenced playing, and the commanding officer led the salute. Jaws dropped in amazement as out onto the red carpet walked the "Big Dogs": ten large, furry huskies used for military reconnaissance.

---★---

From *Leading with My Left*, by Richard Armour (New Leader, 1945)

## GIRDLING FOR WAR

*"Women in Army Corps to Get Two Girdles Each"*
—NEWSPAPER HEADLINE

For girls in service of their nation,
Two girdles are the regulation,

A minimum supply, but still,
Enough, if husbanded with skill,

To last the thrifty Amazon
As long as war is going on.

So, with this taken care of, we
Can hail the coming victory,

In toast to which we lift the cup:
Our woman's army's shaping up!

---

★

---

From *The GI War, 1941–1945,* by Ralph G. Martin (Avon, 1967)

Here's a well-circulated story about an MP ordering the driver of a Marine jeep:

"Put those goddam lights out."

The driver did.

However, the passenger, a general, told the driver, "Put those goddam lights back on."

The driver did.

Now the MP yelled even louder, "Put those goddam lights *out!*"

"I *can't,*" the driver yelled, "I got the goddam general with me!"

---

★

---

From *More G.I. Laughs: Real Army Humor,* selected by Harold Hersey (Sheridan House, 1944)

## GO AHEAD, DEAR!

Do not become a drone, dear,
While I am far away.

Just have a lot of fun, dear,
Step out each night and play.

The lads I left behind, dear,
Must also have their fling.
Be sure to treat them kind, dear,
And dance and laugh and sing.

Do anything you will, dear—
Just pet or flirt or park
With Jack or Joe—with Bill,
Dear, be careful after dark.

The years are too few, dear,
Your happiness to wreck.
But if these things you do, dear,
I'll break your little neck.

———————————————————★———————————————————

From *The Best from* Yank, *the Army Weekly* (Dutton, 1945)

## JILTED GIS IN INDIA ORGANIZE
## FIRST BRUSH-OFF CLUB
by Sergeant Ed Cunningham

AT A U.S. BOMBER BASE, INDIA—For the first time in military history, the mournful hearts have organized. The Brush-Off Club is the result, in this land of sahibs and saris; as usual, it is strictly GI.

Composed of guys whose gals back home have decided "a

few years is too long to wait," the club has only one purpose—to band together for mutual sympathy. They meet weekly to exchange condolences and cry in their beer while telling each other the mournful story of how "she wouldn't wait."

The club has a "chief crier," a "chief sweater," and a "chief consoler." Initiation fee is one broken heart or a reasonable facsimile thereof.

Applicants must be able to answer appropriately the following questions:

- Has she written lately?
- Do her letters say she misses you, and is willing to wait no matter how long?
- Does she reminisce about the "grand times we had together, and the fun we'll have when you come back?"
- Does she mention casually the fellows she is dating now?

Membership is divided between "active members" and "just sweating members"—the latter being guys who can't believe that no news is good news.

Members are required to give each other the needle; i.e., full sympathy for all active members, encourage "hopeful waiting" in the just sweating members. By-laws state: "As we are all in the 'same transport,' we must provide willing shoulders to cry upon, and join fervently in all wailing and weeping."

One of the newest members of the club was unanimously voted to charter membership because of the particular circumstances of his case. He recently got a six-page letter from his fiancée back in Texas. In the last paragraph she casually mentioned, "I was married last week but my husband won't mind you writing to me occasionally. He's a sailor and very broadminded."

This GI, so magnanimously scorned, is now regarded as fine presidential timber.

---

★

---

From *The Best from* Yank, *the Army Weekly* (Dutton, 1945)

## HOW TO GET LOST IN A JUNGLE
by Sergeant Joe McCarthy

Everybody in the Army seems to be writing handy pocket guides these days telling you How to Keep from Getting Lost in a Jungle. These books are all right, but a lot of my friends are not reading them. In the first place, my friends never read anything, anyway, except beer bottle labels and the *Daily Racing Form*. In the second place, my friends are all gold-brickers and they don't want handy pocket guides that tell them how to keep from getting lost. All they want is to *get* lost, as soon as possible.

"The thicker the jungle the better," one of them remarked the other day, squeezing himself into the barrel of his M1 when the first sergeant approached to select a detail.

So my friends have requested, through channels, that I write a piece about How to Get Lost in a Jungle. They couldn't have picked a better man.

I happen to be an expert on getting lost. I spent most of the Carolina Maneuvers in 1941 at the top of the center pole in my pyramidal tent, where nobody could find me when there was a truck to be unloaded. As a matter of fact, I would have beaten Shipwreck Kelly's old record one week but a certain corporal, who shall be nameless, set the tent on fire and smoked me out.

I also happen to be an expert on jungles. I spent most of my summers as a youngster in a jungle near the Gillette razor blade factory in South Boston, Mass.

The first thing to remember if you want to get lost in a jungle is not to lose your head. There are a lot of head hunters in the jungles. If you want to put your head down somewhere for a minute while you are washing your feet or pressing your pants, a head hunter is liable to pick it up and walk off with it.

And don't be afraid of a jungle. A lot of soldiers get nervous when they find themselves in a jungle and notice that it has no traffic lights or sewers. But the jungle is really your friend. It provides heaps and heaps of food which can be found in the form of animals and plants. It also provides malaria, mosquitoes, leeches, snakes, crocodiles, and nettles, but there is no need to go into that now. However, you will be glad to learn that you have much less chance of catching poison ivy in the average jungle than you have around Lake Winnepesaukee, New Hampshire. Here is another bit of good news about jungles: It hardly ever snows there, so the chances are you won't be able to slip on an icy sidewalk and hurt yourself.

I see that the T-5 down there in the fifth row with the Good Conduct ribbon and the whistle has a question. Would you mind speaking a little louder, bully? You say you want to know what kind of food in the jungle is safe to eat?

Well, my fine chowhound, my advice to you is to make

the acquaintanceship of some young monkey about your own age who knows the neighborhood. Just watch what he eats. Then follow his example and you'll make out okay. But be careful about the kind of monkey he is before you start associating with him. Be sure he doesn't drink too much or run around the loose women. Many a careless GI in the jungle has been led to rack and ruin by hanging out with the wrong type of monkey.

Now let me see, where was I?

Oh, yes. The best way to get lost in a jungle is to get rid of your compass. I wouldn't recommend this, however, because the supply sergeant may get nasty and swear out a statement of charges to be deducted from your next month's pay. Pawning the compass wouldn't do either. You might get grabbed for hocking government property and sent to Leavenworth to cool off for a few years. But then again, if you want to look at the bright side of it, Leavenworth is an excellent place to get lost in, too. Even better than a jungle because it has no malaria mosquitoes.

I find the best way to get lost is to ask directions from an MP. Simply go where he tells you to go and, in no time at all, you won't have the slightest idea of where you are.

But be careful about crossing state lines. Even though we are at war, don't forget that they are still able to get you for violations of the Mann Act.

That covers about everything except malaria mosquitoes and the natives. The best remedy for mosquitoes is to burn punks. This is getting rather difficult to do now because most of the punks in the Army have either gone to OCS or have been released under the 38-year-old law.

There is no need to try to cover the natives. They have

been walking around without clothes all their lives, so you can't expect them to do anything different.

In closing, I suggest that you bring this page with you next time you feel like getting lost in a jungle. It might come in handy to light a fire with.

---

★

---

From *Artie Greengroin, Pfc.*, by Harry Brown (Knopf, 1945)

"I ain't one to complain," Artie said, "but I wish they'd not of sent me to the English Isle." Artie was sitting in the kitchen, his legs wrapped around a huge cauldron of unpeeled potatoes. In another, much smaller cauldron lay the seven he had succeeded in peeling in the last hour. Artie for the thousandth time was on KP. He was as browned off as a frying-pan full of home-fries.

I lounged against a door, moodily eating a raw cauliflower, watching Artie lay on with the knife. "Maybe you'd like it better in Labrador," I suggested.

"Maybe I would," Artie said. "I got some very good reasons to like Labrador. In the foist place, it's a unfertile country. Nothing grows there, nothing but ice. You don't find no pertaters in Labrador. Everything comes out of the can. They's no KP. They's no work at all."

"You heard of Maine and Idaho?" I asked.

"Yeah. States," said Artie.

"Well," I said, "they take potatoes from Maine and Idaho and they put them on boats and they send them up to Labrador for those boys to peel."

Artie's eyes widened. "They do?" he said. "Why, the doity

ole bassars. Thass all they do, make our life a hell. You'd think once they get a bunch of Joes up in Labrador they'd say: 'Well, them boys is having a hard time up there with all that ice and stuff, we jess won't send 'em no pertaters to peel.' Thass what you'd think they'd say, huh? But what do they do? They toin right around and give you a hit on the udder cheek. What a war!"

Artie took a vicious cut at a fresh potato, nearly severing it in half.

"Take your time," I said.

"Why don't you give me a hand with these pertaters?" Artie asked.

"It's against my religion," I said.

"Thass gratitude, after all I done for you," Artie said. "Thass some gratitude. I been making your life easier ever since I run into you. I took pity on you, thass what I did. And these is my thanks."

"They sure are," I said.

"Thass what I get for helping a fellow man on the life of ease," Artie said. "I'm going to toin into a hoimet and get away from the humane race. Maybe if I got me a transfer to India, things would be different."

"They'd be hotter," I said.

"They's nothing like slipping a body into a nice, cool hunk of khaki," Artie said. "Thass the way they do things in India. In India a Pfc. is really something. You go out and hire somebody to make your bed and give the ole shine to yer shoes and you jess lie on the veranda and wet your whistle. You want to enjoy the Army, go to India."

I said I wouldn't enjoy the Army wherever I was.

"It jess goes to show," Artie said. "Thass what comes of

being a soft apple. A man's got to be able to acclimate himself. I acclimate very well. If I was shipped to India tomorrer, I would slip into the life of ease like a native. I can get used to a fruit diet jess like anything else. There's no pertaters in India."

"You forgot about those ships?" I wanted to know.

Artie dropped the potato he was working on. "Ah, you don't mean it," he said. You don't mean to tell me they send them ships full of pertaters all the way to India?"

"That's what I mean," I said.

"Well, I'll be the son of a first sergeant," Artie said. "Honest to gaw, what them ole bassars won't do. It makes me boin, honest to gaw." He picked up the potato he had been working on and threw it out the open window. "They jess ain't no place in this whole woild thass sacred to leisure, is they?"

"You hit the spike on the cephalos," I said.

"Yeah," Artie said, "ain't it the truth? Well, thass jess another dream busted. Jess another dream. I ain't got many of them left these days."

The vast hulk of the mess sergeant loomed up at the window. "Who trun that spud?"

Artie looked at him casually. "Oh, hullo, sergeant," he said. "I'm going like a house afire. These pertaters is a breeze. Nothing to it at all, sergeant."

The mess sergeant is probably the only man in the world of whom Artie is afraid. To him the mess sergeant is the whole German Army, a death ray, the Blue Beetle, Submariner, and God knows what else, all rolled into one.

"Who trun that spud?" the mess sergeant asked.

"Is somebody trunning pertaters?" Artie said. "Thass a

hell of a thing to do. It's a mug's game, trunning pertaters."

"Greengroin," the mess sergeant said, "I got my eye on you. And I got a gleam in my eye. And the gleam ain't doing you no good."

"Sergeant," Artie said, "in this Army nothing does you no good."

"Trapped, huh?" said the mess sergeant.

"Yerse," Artie said.

"Who trun that spud?" said the mess sergeant.

"You mean out of the winder?" Artie asked.

"Thass what I mean," said the mess sergeant.

"Maybe it was me," Artie said. "Was it me?" he asked me.

"It was you," I said.

"I was carried away by a subjeck I was conversing with," Artie said.

"Greengroin, yer a no-good," the mess sergeant said. "Was the subjeck you was conversing with KP by any chancet?"

"It was the subjeck of the life of ease," Artie said.

"Well, all I got to say at this very moment," the mess sergeant said, "is that it's too bad it wasn't KP, because KP is a subjeck you are going to be very conversing on, because you are going to be doing KP for the next week if you can be spared, and I got a feeling you can be spared."

With that the vast bulk of the mess sergeant disappeared from the window. With a sigh, Artie turned back to his work. "Honest to gaw," he said, "do they really send pertaters all the way to India?"

They clutch at straws, do drowning men.

———————————————— ★ ————————————————

From *The Stars and Stripes: World War II and the Early Years*, by Ken Zumwalt (Eakins Press, 1989)

On Saturday, December 20 [1944, *The Stars and Stripes*] reported that Gen. George S. Patton's 3rd Army had retaken thirteen towns and his 4th Armored Division, which broke the siege of Bastogne, was pouring into that city and widening the corridor.

On the back page . . . was a box which said:

"GIVE UP," SAID NAZIS;
"NUTS!" SAID GENERAL

"When the Germans demanded the surrender of the American forces holding besieged Bastogne, the 101st Airborne's acting commander, Brig. Gen. Anthony C. McAuliffe, according to the Associated Press, gave the enemy one of the briefest replies in military history.

" 'Nuts,' he said."

Three days later there was another box pertaining to McAuliffe's comment, and this one rightly made the front page.

NO COMPRIS "NUTS,"
SAY PARIS PAPERS

"The French press was full of praise for the American stand at Bastogne but it was a little baffled by the word 'Nuts' with which Brig. Gen. Anthony C. McAuliffe rejected the Germans demand for surrender.

" '*Vous n'êtes que de vieilles noix,*' was the way Paris papers rendered it: 'You are nothing but old nuts.'

"'This phrase,' wrote *L'Aurore*'s New York correspondent, 'is entered in the American vocabulary forever.'

"*C'est vrai!*"

McAuliffe made it clear in a press conference that the 101st Airborne Division was not "rescued" at Bastogne.

"Anyone who says we were rescued or who thinks we needed rescue is all wrong. On Christmas night, I called my regimental commanders together and told them we now were ready for pursuit."

The text of his reply to the Germans was terse:

> *22 Dec. 44 To The German Commander:*
> *N-U-T-S. (Signed) American Commander.*

---

★

---

From *c/o Postmaster*, by Corporal Thomas R. St. George (Thomas Y. Crowell Co., 1943)

*Corporal St. George and his platoon found themselves stationed in various parts of Australia.*

Living as we did, so far from civilization, we grew to rely solely on the United States Army Service Forces for all our wants. And we found out what happened to the little boys who threw rocks at the blind newsboy—they'd grown up, joined the Army, and gone to work in the canteens. And now they had at their fingertips all the things we desired. Soap, shaving cream, razor blades, cigarettes, matches, Coca-Cola, everything that could be classed as a luxury, these thugs controlled. They were in a position to bully. And whether we liked it or them or not, we must needs be nice to them. So we were nice to them, friendly as all hell, in fact. BUT WHEN THIS WAR IS OVER. . . . As Sergeant Rubtikish put it: "You think those bastards was buyin' that stuff with their own money, an' tryin' to save everything they ever had."

Except for the personnel involved (and an overabundance of inventories), our canteens were a wonderful institution, taking the place of the Salvation Army, the Post Service Club, the local pub, and the still nonexistent U.S.O. They dispensed ice cream in three flavors and ice-cold Coca-Cola. Taking these ingredients back to our tents, we would mix them and drink "frosted cokes" while writing home describing our bare existence in the middle of the God-forsaken bush.

Beer, too, was G.I. Usually we received a ration of three bottles per man once a week, any known teetotalers being approached days in advance of "beer night" with wild offers of almost anything in any quantity would they only "lemme have your beer this week." We learned that beer can be appreciated and enjoyed without being served by a blonde barmaid having a nice pair of legs.

Laundry, as always, was a bit of a problem. Sent out every other Tuesday, it came back—IF it came back—a week or so after all concerned had just about given up hope and opened a campaign with the supply sergeant for some new clothes. When it did come, it came by the truckload and was dumped wholesale in the supply tent, where those who could convince anybody they'd sent laundry were allowed to paw through the mess until they found whatever it was they'd sent or a reasonable facsimile thereof. Naturally, everybody went in with the idea that come what might *he* would "find" at least as many clothes as he'd sent away. Soldiers who were approximately the same size watched each other closely, suspiciously, like hawks, at all times; and it was sheer folly to reach for a size "30" anything while another size "30" was looking on.

When it came to amusing ourselves we had the usual games of chance, the regimental band, and movies. However, our company neither approved of nor appreciated the regimental band. This organization was quartered next to us and from very early in the morning until very late at night they practiced a variety of tunes on a variety of instruments, never more than four of them on the same tune, but all favoring heavy bass notes that made the trees quiver. They ate with us, too, which made our chow line considerably longer, but were excused from furnishing any K.P.'s, another unending source of hate. We discussed all kinds of sabotage that we might wreak on the band. Particularly, we wanted to pour sand in the bass horn.

Sometimes, of course, the band did furnish us with a certain amount of entertainment. Otherwise, we relied on our cinema, which, like the best in the States, had stars on the roof. As a matter of fact, the stars *were* the roof. Mostly the pictures themselves appeared to have been knocked out by Hollywood in something less than thirty-six hours for a cost of not more than seventy-five dollars including the premiere, but they were still movies. And we were still fans. Generally, each picture was shown three nights running and we attended three nights running, until some of us who had also seen the same feature a couple of times in civilian life could, with little or no effort, repeat all the punch lines from memory. Naturally enough, certain characters *did* repeat all the punch lines from memory, usually just prior to their appearing on the screen. We cheered madly when a familiar place or the old home state was mentioned. To a man, it seemed, we shrieked and whistled if a silk-clad feminine leg so much as flashed across the screen. We longed for those good old-fashioned newsreels full of sweepstakes winners and bathing beauties instead of London's latest blitz. We watched Travelogues of Tahiti and Havana ("The Pearl of the Caribbean") and Tasmania and Old Mexico and wished that just once Mr. Fitzpatrick had gone to Kalamazoo.

All in all, we liked our "staging area" better than we had liked our "bloody resort plice," but we were still a long ways from home—a hell of a long ways from home—and overwhelmingly anxious and eager to see something, anything, that reminded us of the Main Streets we had known "back in the States."

★

From *The Best from* Yank, *the Army Weekly* (Dutton, 1945)

## A SACK OF MAIL
by Corporal Paul E. Deutschmann

SOMEWHERE IN SARDINIA—Mail call is one of the most important things in a GI's life, I was reading the other day. It's good for that ethereal something that USO hostesses, advertising copywriters, and sundry other civilians back home call morale. With the correspondents some GIs have, though, no mail is good mail. Leave us look at some of these morale-boosters.

### Fidgety-Filly Type

"Snookie, dear—I drove out to Petter's Perch the other night, along the Old Mill Road. You remember, don't you, dear? The moon was bright and the stars twinkled just like when you were there with me, and it made me feel so-o-o romantic!

"Some girls complain about the man shortage. But not me! Last night three fellows took me to the movies, and afterwards they took turns with me out on the back porch—dancing. But don't worry, dear, they were all servicemen. I won't go out with a man except in uniform. One of them, Casper Clutchem, who is sorta blond and cute and a Marine sergeant, says for me to tell you 'the situation is under control.' He is *awful* strong.

"Guess what we were drinking? Those potent daquiris. They really make me forget myself—almost.

"And did I tell you? Casper is stationed just outside of town and has promised to come see me real often. I couldn't very well refuse him because he said he was leaving for overseas almost any month now. I believe in doing my bit to help the servicemen because, after all, some of them are so far from home and don't know a soul in town."

### Home-Guard Type

"Dear Corp—I am back in Dayton for another furlough and I am looking after Lulu, just like you asked me to. She's really a wonderful gal and a smooth dancer. And if she weren't your wife I could really go for her myself. Do you realize I've gotten to know Lulu better than you do—almost! And boy, can she hold her likker!

"We had dinner at the Cove tonight and are now back at your apartment. It is just midnight and while Lulu is slipping into something more *comfortable*, I thought I'd drop you a line. Ha ha, old man, I'm only kidding."

## Man-of-Affairs Type

"I've been doing swell at the office. Just got the Whatsis Soap and Whoozis Hosiery account. That's $4,000,000 billing besides the pleasure I get from interviewing models for the 'leg art' pictures. But it's nothing like the swell job you boys are doing over there. I wish I were in there with you but——

"Give 'em hell for me, old fellow! They asked for it—and we're just the guys to give it to them. I'm buying War Bonds like an insane stamp collector. I really wish I were out in the foxholes with you, but——"

## Civilian Brass-Hat Type

"Dear Bill—All of us here at the Old Company, from the office staff up to me, are thinking of you boys in the service and doing our part to help you fellas. We're all buying War Bonds and cutting down on meat and butter—and some of the girls in the office are even rolling bandages on Saturday afternoons, when they aren't working.

"Rationing is pretty grim now. Steaks only twice a week and no more cherries in cherry cokes. But we don't mind because the papers say that you fellows overseas are getting all the good things—and you certainly deserve them.

"Yes sir, no one can say that the Old Company is not well represented in the foxholes and trenches of our fighting fronts all over the globe. Rollie is a warrant officer at Camp Dix, N.J., and Jim is at the Brooklyn Navy Yard, and Harry is the chauffeur to a Marine colonel in Philadelphia. Van is way down in Texas and Charlie is a quartermaster clerk in Georgia and you're in the Infantry in Italy. Give 'em hell, boy."

### Oh-You-Devil Type

"You guys over there in Italy must be having a big time with all those little dark-eyed signorinas. Do they wear those grass skirts like Dorothy Lamour?"

### Local-Boy-Makes-Good Type

"Your cousin Herman is now a technical sergeant and he has only been in the Army five months. I can't understand why you're still a corporal. Are your officers mad at you?"

### All-In-This-Together Type

"Dear Pal—Things are really getting rugged now at good old Camp Kilmer. I can only get off every other weekend. We went out on bivouac last week and, boy, was it rough! We slept in pup tents for three nights—right on the ground.

"Last week I was awarded the Good Conduct Ribbon at a special ceremony. You might not hear from me for a while, as I am expecting to be shipped out any day now—to North Carolina.

"By the way—what is this Spam we hear so much about?"

---

★

---

From *The GI War, 1941–1945*, by Ralph G. Martin (Avon, 1967)

[During] the usual [grueling] banzai charges on Guam, some Marines even kidded about them, passing out this mimeographed announcement.

TONIGHT
BANZAI CHARGE
*Thrills    Chills    Suspense*
*See Sake-Crazed Japanese Charge at High Port*
*See Everybody Shoot Everybody*
*See the Cream of the Marine Corps Play with Live Ammo*
*Sponsored by the Athletic and Morale Office*
*Come Along and Bring a Friend*
*Don't Miss the Thrilling Spectacle of the Banzai Charge*
*Starting at 10 p.m. and Lasting All Night*
ADMISSION FREE

──────────────── ★ ────────────────

An army transport was a week out of New York City, and running without lights in the submarine zone. Some of the guys were playing poker. In the midst of some friendly kicking and re-kicking, there was a mighty impact against the boat. All was quiet for a few seconds, then a voice shouted: "We're torpedoed!"

All the poker players but one leapt to their feet.

"Hey, wait, you guys!" cried the fellow who'd remained seated. "You can't leave me now, I've got four aces!"

──────────────── ★ ────────────────

From *Up Front*, by Bill Mauldin (Henry Holt & Co., 1945)

As long as you've got to have an Army you've got to have officers, so you might as well make the most of it.

The ideal officer in any army knows his business. He is firm and just. He is saluted and given the respect due a man who knows enough about war to boss soldiers around in it. He is given many privileges, which all officers are happy to accept and he is required, in return, to give certain things which a few officers choose to ignore. I try to make life as miserable as possible for those few.

An officer is not supposed to sleep until his men are bedded down. He is not supposed to eat until he has arranged for his men to eat. He's like a prizefighter's manager. If he keeps his fighter in shape the fighter will make him successful. I respect those combat officers who feel this responsibility so strongly that many of them are killed fulfilling it.

Since I am an enlisted man, and have served under many officers, I have a great deal of respect for the good ones and a great deal of contempt for the bad ones. A man accepts a commission with his eyes open and, if he does not intend to take responsibilities as well as privileges, he is far lower than the buck private who realizes his own limitations and keeps that rank.

I never worry about hurting the feelings of the good officers when I draw officer cartoons. I build a shoe, and if somebody wants to put it on and loudly announce that it fits, that's his own affair.

A few of them have done it, to the subsequent enjoyment of

"*Beautiful view. Is there one for the enlisted men?*"

the guys who read the letters to the editor in the Mail Call section of *Stars and Stripes*. One poor lieutenant—let's call him Smith to be on the safe side—wrote that instead of picking on officers, I should stop and consider the stupid antics of enlisted men whom he had observed in his three years' service. Several letters came back—not defending me, but putting the blast on the lieutenant for being foolish enough to call soldiers stupid. I remember one of the letters very well. It began:

> "... *I pick up the October 23rd issue of* Stars and Stripes *and what do I see but a letter from my old pal, Lt. Smith. The last I heard from 'Stinky' Smith, he was studying for his third attempt to make a score of 110 in his General Classification test in order to qualify for OCS. . . . Now, 'Stinky,' when you worked in my poultry house in 1940, picking turkeys for $14 a week, neither myself nor the other boys regarded you as a mental giant. Quite the contrary. . . ."*

This undoubtedly provided the boys in Lieutenant Smith's outfit with considerable glee.

Once a British friend on the Eighth Army paper asked me why I didn't draw something about them. So I did.

There was a standing joke for a while between the British division at Anzio and one of the American divisions. The Americans, noted for their wealth of matériel, often littered the area with discarded equipment, and the thrifty British who relieved them just couldn't understand it. If a British colonel draws an unnecessary pair of shoes for his regimental supply, he's likely to get a court-martial out of it, and God help the Tommy who loses his Enfield rifle.

*"You blokes leave an awfully messy battlefield."*

So the British used to accuse the Americans of leaving a messy battlefield, and I drew a picture of a Tommy telling that to two dogfaces. The British up there seemed to like it okay, and the doggies at Anzio caught it. But the British brass in Naples made a complaint. They didn't understand the picture, but they were certain it was anti-British.

I was sorry that happened, because I think the offended ones belonged to a minority, and the British would have given me quite a lot of opportunities for cartooning.

Their drivers are a little trouble sometimes, because they can't get used to the right-hand side of the highways, and they are often cussed at by our guys. Their brass hats are very stuffy, like a lot of ours, and I think it would have been a pleasure to work on them.

If you can get behind an Englishman's unholy fear of making a friend until he has known the candidate for at least five years, you will find him a pretty good egg. . . .

The attitude of the dogface toward America and the home front is a complex thing. Nobody loves his own land more than a soldier overseas, and nobody swears at it more. He loves it because he appreciates it after seeing the horrible mess that has been made of Europe.

He has seen . . . stark fear and utter destruction and horrible hunger. But at the same time he has seen families bravely trying to rebuild their shattered homes, and he has seen husbands and wives with rifles fighting ahead of him in France. He knows how they can throw themselves completely and unselfishly into the war when it is necessary.

So he is naturally going to get sore when he thinks of

selfishness at home. He got just as sore at the big company which was caught bribing inspectors and sending him faulty armor for his tanks as he did at the workers who held up production in vital factories. He doesn't have time to go into economics and labor-management problems. All he knows is that he is expected to make great sacrifices for little compensation, and he must make those sacrifices whether he likes it or not. Don't expect him to weigh the complicated problem before he gets sore. He knows he delivered and somebody else didn't.

But, in spite of these irritations, the soldier's pride in his country is immense. He's proud of the splendid equipment he gets from home, and sometimes he even gets a little overbearing about it.

Often soldiers who are going home say they are going to tell the people how fortunate we were to stop the enemy before he was able to come and tear up our country. They are also going to tell the people that it is a pretty rough life over here.

I've tried to do that in my drawings and I know that many thousands of guys who have gone back home have tried to do it, too. But no matter how much we try we can never give the folks at home any idea of what war really is. I guess you have to go through it to understand its horrors. You can't understand it by reading magazines or newspapers or by looking at pictures or by going to newsreels. You have to smell it and feel it all around you until you can't imagine what it used to be like when you walked on a sidewalk or tossed clubs up into horse chestnut trees or fished for perch or when you did anything at all without a pack, a rifle, and a bunch of grenades.

We all used to get sore at some of the ads we saw in magazines from America. The admen should have been required by law to submit all copy to an overseas veteran before they sent it to the printers.

I remember one lulu of a refrigerator ad showing a lovely, dreamy-eyed wife gazing across the blue seas and reflecting on how much she misses Jack . . . BUT she knows he'll never be content to come back to his cozy nest (equipped with a Frosty refrigerator; sorry, we're engaged in vital war production now) until the Hun is whipped and the world is clean for Jack's little son to grow up in.

Chances are that Jack, after eighteen or twenty months of combat, is rolling his eyes and making gurgling sounds every time the company commander comes around, so the old man will think he is battle-happy and send him home on rotation. Like hell Jack doesn't want to come home now.

And when he does come home you can bet he'll buy some other brand of refrigerator with his demobilization pay, just to spite the Frosty adman.

Those who look carefully at newspaper pictures have probably observed that many Germans are captured at the front without helmets, while our guys wear them almost all the time. One of the reasons for this is that we were taught very thoroughly that a helmet is a good thing to have around, but the main reason is because the American helmet is a handy instrument even when you're not wearing it. You can dig with it, cook with it, gather fruit with it, and bathe with it. The only disadvantage of the helmet is that it is drafty in winter and hot in summer.

# MESS AND
# OTHER GRUB

From *See Here, Private Hargrove*, by Marion Hargrove (Henry Holt, 1942)

It was through no fault of mine that I was a kitchen police-man on my sixth day [in the service]. The whole barracks got the grind. And it was duty, not punishment.

It was all very simple, this KP business. All you have to do is get up an hour earlier, serve the food, and keep the mess hall clean.

After we served breakfast, I found a very easy job in the dining hall, where life is much pinker than it is in the kitchen. A quartet was formed and we were singing "Home on the Range." A corporal passed by just as I hit a sour note. He put the broom into my right hand, the mop into my left. . . .

There was a citizen-soldier from Kannapolis to help me clean the cooks' barracks. For a time it was awful. We tried to concentrate on the floor while a news broadcaster almost tore up the radio trying to decide whether we were to be in the Army ten years or twenty.

We finished the job in an extremely short time to impress the corporal. This, we found later, is a serious tactical blunder and a discredit to the ethics of goldbricking. The sooner you finish a job the sooner you start on the next.

The corporal liked our work, unfortunately. Kannapolis was allowed to sort garbage and I was promoted to the pot-and-pan polishing section. I was Thomas Kokene's assistant. He washed and I dried. Later we formed a goldbricking entente. We both washed and made Conrad Wilson dry.

Pollyanna the glad girl would have found something silver-lined about the hot sink. So did I. "At least," I told Kokenes, "this will give my back a chance to recover from that mop."

When I said "mop," the mess sergeant handed me one. He wanted to be able to see his face in the kitchen floor. After lunch he wanted the back porch polished.

We left the Reception Center mess hall a better place to eat in, at any rate. But KP is like women's work—never really done. Conrad Wilson marked one caldron and at the end of the day we found that we had washed it twenty-two times.

Jack Mulligan helped me up the last ten steps to the squadroom. I finally got to the side of my bunk. "Gentlemen," I said to the group which gathered around to scoop me off the floor, "I don't ever want to see another kitchen!"

The next morning we were classified and assigned to the Field Artillery Replacement Center. Gene Shumate and I were classified as cooks. I am a semi-skilled cook, they say, although the only egg I ever tried to fry was later used as a tire patch. The other cooks include former postal clerks, tractor salesmen, railroad engineers, riveters, bricklayers, and one blacksmith.

But we'll learn. Already I've learned to make beds, sweep, mop, wash windows, and sew a fine seam. When Congress lets me go home, will I make some woman a good wife!

Salt pork, which you rarely see in the Army, is called lamb chop. "They lam it against the wall to get the salt out of it and then they chop it up into the beans."

---

★

---

"Did you say you wanted those eggs turned over?" the mess cook asked the private.

"Yeah," came the reply. "To the Museum of Natural History."

---

★

---

A rookie passing the mess hall asked the head cook, "Say, what's on the menu tonight?"

"Oh, we have thousands of things to eat tonight," replied the cook.

"What are they?"

"Beans!"

---

★

---

From *The Best from* Yank, *the Army Weekly* (Dutton, 1945)

## NOMENCLATURE OF THE PACKAGE, APO
by Corporal James O'Neill

SOMEWHERE IN THE PERSIAN GULF—Now that the Army Postal Service has restored the soldier's privilege of getting packages from home, we would like to commend the APS for putting in the clause which says the soldier must ask for a package to get it.

This requirement . . . is not, as some believe, an effort to limit the number of packages. It springs from the demands of soldiers that they be protected against the parcel post system. Reports show that the first AEF in Ireland as long as a year ago was actually sabotaging incoming box-laden boats by purposely not claiming title to the merchandise at time of delivery.

This practice spread until thousands of boxes lay purposely unclaimed on wharves all over the combatant world, and the Army Postal Service probably conducted an investigation to discover why. The APS no doubt discovered the reason: No soldier would claim a package because (a) he knew what was in it, (b) he had had enough of what was in it, or (c) even his worst enemy and first sergeant had had enough of what was in it. .

From now on we get an even break with the people who make up packages. We get to tell them what to put in.

Up to this time there have been only four variations of the box-sending theme.

Let us discuss them, now that they are a thing of the past:

## Type A: The Goodie Box

Invariably consisted of two items—candy or home-made cookies. There were two choices open to the unfortunate recipient of home-made cookies. He could, if still in love and his sweetheart sent them, try to eat the cookies. This lovelorn type cabled home the next day for a new upper plate and a stomach pump. If the guy wasn't in love or just didn't give a damn, he took the sensible course of donating love's handiwork to the Engineers for road markers or dummy land mines.

## Type B—Gooey-Yum-Yum Kandy Kit

En route the kit was placed by considerate stevedores between the engine room boilers and a shipment of Grant tanks. When the soldier received it, he could use the mashed-up goo for pasting French postcards or *Yank* pin-ups on his barracks wall. Or if he had a little goat's blood in him, he might start right in eating Gooey-Yum-Yum's wrappings, partitions, string, APO number and all.

Suppose the sender was the thoughtful type and sent hard candy that stayed hard. Tell me who in hell is going to sacrifice his native-likker-weakened molars on a job a couple of Grant tanks couldn't do? The ingenious AAF is said to be using these dextrose blockbusters over Berlin, the only practical use so far discovered.

## Type C—The Knit-One-and-Purl-One Box

The sort of box that caused the recent high female death rate by accidental self-stabbing. It contained The Knitted Glove or The Knitted Pullover Sweater. Already enough has been said on this gruesome subject in newspaper editorials, syndicated columns, joke books, and returned packages marked "Wrong Address."

### Type D—The Odds-and-Ends Box

This always fell into one of the following subdivisions:

1. *The Sewing Kit.* This was the 1,442nd one the helpless GI received. Despite all the Boy Scout and Sewing Kit Concession propaganda, the average GI doesn't know how to sew. Even if he did, Whistler's Mother couldn't darn the craters he plows through a sock. Upon receipt of the sewing kit, the soldier carefully took out the needles to pin up that picture of Jane Russell and threw the rest away.

2. *The Compact Shaving Kit.* This monster was delivered by a detail of 10 and, when opened, resembled a surgeon's operating room, complete with X-ray equipment. It so scared the dogface that he refused to shave with anything for a month.

3. *The Photograph.* Usually sent by that much-maligned creature, the Girl Back Home, who, unless she was straight out of *Vogue*, included an original little note, "Put this in the mess hall to scare the rats away." It could do the job very well. If the girl was a looker, she had had the picture taken with one of the boys back home "just to make you feel a teeny-weeny bit jealous." The guy looked like Cary Grant and was either sporting a pair of oak leaves or clutching a $1,000 war-industry check in one hand.

4. *The Canned Tidbit.* Usually tied in a maze of fancy ribbon, this was something the dogface hopefully ripped open with anxious hands only to discover a can of Spam. (Last week the mess sergeant was clubbed to death with empty cans that had contained this ersatz chicken.)

Now that us soldiers overseas are allowed to select that contents of our packages from home, here are four types of gift boxes that we would like to receive:

A—One Lana Turner and one case of Scotch.
B—One Dinah Shore and one case of Scotch.
C—One Rita Hayworth and one case of Scotch.
D—One Scotch and one case of Jane Russells.

This lyric, often sung, appraised the quality of coffee generally available to servicemen:

> *The coffee that they give us*
> *They say is mighty fine.*
> *It's good for cuts and bruises*
> *In place of iodine.*

---

★

---

From *The GI War, 1941–1945*, by Ralph G. Martin (Avon, 1967)

The food was . . . not to everybody's taste. One of the lesser delights for breakfast was creamed beef on toast, more popularly known as SOS—sh*t on a shingle.

Somebody found this instruction in Training Manual 10-405, *The Army Cook:*

"There is no limit to what can be done to improve a mess by thought and care and seasoning, attractive serving, and inventing new combinations and mixtures of foods. The pleasant task of cooking becomes doubly interesting to the cook who is not satisfied with merely cooking well, but takes advantage of every opportunity of finding new and pleasing ways to prepare food. To him, cooking is not just a task—it is a pleasure.

"Good cooking is recognized the world over as a fine art, and a good cook commands respect. Cooks who perfect themselves in their art are always in demand and many have acquired wealth and fame."

Everybody thought this was as funny as Bob Hope.

---

★

---

Contributed to *Reader's Digest*'s "Humor in Uniform" by J. F. Carithers

I was stationed on Leyte during World War II. Although the region was secure, sometimes the enemy tried to infiltrate our food storage area. One such adversary, dressed in GI clothing, once worked himself into the noontime chow line. Our camp cook spotted him, reached under the serving table for his pistol, and yelled for the MPs who were patrolling the area.

After it was all over, we asked the cook how he knew the man was an enemy soldier. "I figured it wasn't one of you guys," he said, " 'cause he was coming back for seconds."

---

★

---

From *Up Front*, by Bill Mauldin (Henry Holt & Co., 1945)

A couple of infantry sat on a mountain in Italy in mud, rain, snow, and freezing cold weather. They had inadequate clothing and they didn't get relief. They sat there for weeks, and the only men who came down the mountain were dead ones, badly wounded ones, and those who had trench foot from the icy mud.

During that entire period, the dogfaces didn't have a hot meal. Sometimes they had little gasoline stoves and were able to heat packets of "predigested" coffee, but most often they did it with matches—hundreds of matches which barely took the chill off the brew. Soon the guys ran out of matches.

Because they were on K rations they had coffee only once a day. The dinner ration had synthetic lemonade—a mixture of carbolic acid and ersatz lemon powder. Try drinking that in a muddy foxhole in freezing weather. The supper ration had a sort of bouillon soup, which was impossible. It takes a lot of water to make it, and a lot more to drown the salty thirst it causes. Usually there wasn't even enough water for the guys to brush their teeth because there weren't enough mules to haul it up.

Our army is pretty well fed behind the lines—as well fed as an army can be. The food advertisers who show a soldier wallowing in goodies aren't far wrong. The abundance of food in our big ration dumps amazes Europeans. But the advertisers make one mistake. They always show the solider wallowing in goodies at the front. He doesn't wallow in anything but mud up there.

Usually it's nobody's fault. In Sicily and Southern France

things moved so fast it was hard for the supplies to catch up. In Italy the mountains complicated the supply situation.

Since there is not much a cook can do while his company is in combat, his worth depends upon how many ration cases he can carry and not upon how flaky his corn bread turns out. Occasionally a few cooks managed to get hot food up to their boys, but this didn't happen very often.

Front-line troops got K and C rations because the bulky B units, which contain fruit juice, flour for pastries, and all the nice things a guy likes to eat, were too much for the mules which had to carry everything else, including ammunition and water. The main trouble with K and C rations was their monotony. I suppose they had all the necessary calories and vitamins, but they didn't fill your stomach and you got awfully tired of them.

It's a tragedy that all the advantages of being in the American Army never get to those who need them most—the men at the front. It was the same with the Red Cross and movies and all the rest of the better things. You just can't have variety shows and movie screens at the front.

. . . While the rule books probably frown on it, there are few soldiers who haven't traded army rations for civilian food when it was available. It's funny to watch a civilian, sick of his potato soup, brown bread, and red wine, wolf one of those horrible K rations as eagerly as the soldier tears into the soup and bread and wine.

. . . One of my best friends is a cook in an infantry company when he's not in the klink. I once drove him back to a ration dump to get a sack of flour. He wanted to make pancakes for his boys, who hadn't seen pancakes for seven months. I told the guys at the ration dump that I was scrounging for *Stars and Stripes*, and that we wanted to do a story, with photographs, about the men who work in ration dumps. They fell for it, and didn't even stop to wonder why in hell *Stars and Stripes* wanted a sack of flour. We got the sack but those ration men are still looking for their pictures in the paper.

Halfway back to the company area, Mike remembered that we hadn't asked for baking soda. We went back, but they didn't have any soda. Then Mike asked for a few cases of tooth powder, and we got that. After Mike got back to the company, every guy had all the pancakes he could eat. They were made with GI tooth powder, and, in spite of the recipe, they tasted pretty good.

That's how the infantry gets along most of the time.

# R & R

An American soldier had been on the front lines in Europe for three months, when he was finally given a week of R&R.

He caught a supply boat to a supply base in the south of England, then caught a train to London. The train was extremely crowded and he could not find a seat. He was dead on his feet, so he walked the length of the train looking for any place to sit down.

Finally he found a small compartment with seats facing each other; there was room for two people on each seat. On one side sat only a proper-looking, older British lady, with a small dog sitting in the empty seat beside her.

"Could I please sit in that seat?" he asked.

The lady was insulted. "Certainly not! You Americans are so rude," she said, "can't you see my dog is sitting there"?

He walked through the train once more and still could not find a seat.

He found himself back at the same place.

"Lady, I love dogs—I've got a couple of my own back

home—so I would be more than glad to hold your dog if I could just sit down."

The lady replied, "You Americans are not only rude, you are arrogant."

He leaned against the wall for a time, but was so tired he finally said, "Lady, I've been on the front lines in Europe for three months with not a decent rest during all that time. Could I please sit there and hold your dog?"

The lady replied, "You Americans are not only rude and arrogant, you are also obnoxious."

With that comment, the soldier calmly stepped in, picked up the dog, threw it out the window, and sat down.

The woman was utterly speechless.

An older, nattily dressed Englishman sitting across on the other seat spoke up. "Young man, I have no idea whether all you Americans fit the lady's description of you or not. But I do know that you Americans do a lot of things wrong. You drive on the wrong side of the road, you hold your fork with the wrong hand, and now you have just thrown the wrong bitch out of the window."

---

★

---

Following duty overseas, some officers at the Fort were planning a welcome home dance for the unit. Being an all-male combat force, they decided to request coeds from some of the surrounding colleges to attend.

The Captain called Vassar and was assured by the Dean that arrangements could be made to send over a dozen of their most trustworthy students.

The Captain hesitated, then said, "Would it also be possible to send a dozen or so of the other kind?"

---

★

---

From *The Best from* Yank, *the Army Weekly* (Dutton, 1945)

## IRAN COOTIES SHARE TOP BILLING
## WITH MARX BROTHERS AT THE MOVIES
by Sergeant Al Hine

TEHERAN, IRAN—If you're smart, you go to the GI movie in camp. But you're not smart—yet. So you try your luck at one of the half-dozen cinemas in town. Cinema comes from a Greek word meaning move, which is what you do before the feature is half-over.

You begin quite undramatically paying for your ticket—10 *rials* to the wall-eyed girl in the ticket cage. Your ticket is a flimsy bit of colored paper something like the revenue stamp on a whisky bottle. After it has been torn in half by the three-year-old ticket taker, it is like nothing.

The evening's entertainment opens with news reels in French, Russian, and Persian. Very interesting for Frenchmen, Russians, and Persians. The news reels are followed by colored lantern slides advertising cafes, hair lotions, and the *Agence de Publicité* which prepares them. Then the feature.

*The Big Store* with the Marx Brothers (you saw it back in Topeka, back when you got in for half-price as a minor) boasts some scratchy English dialogue. It takes a minute or so before you notice that a running commentary in French is being flashed on the bottom of the screen. It doesn't matter whether you understand French or not; you still keep glancing down curiously at this phenomenon, missing a good part of the action and the English dialogue as well.

After a little concentration, you master the technique. You ignore the French and apply your talents exclusively to the mangled English. You are going along swimmingly when the film flickers to a stop. The Brothers Marx are replaced by a blank white space, which is soon covered with black Persian script explaining the action so far. Persian is a tedious tongue and it takes a full ten minutes to tell what happened in five minutes of screen action.

The Marx Brothers take over once more. You have lost track of the continuity but fortunately, with the Marx Brothers, that doesn't matter much. Back in the swing, you are just trying to remember what it was you laughed at so hard in Topeka when the film stops again.

This time it's an intermission of sorts. A corporal's guard of white-coated urchins pads along the rows, selling chocolate, coffee, gum drops, and, for all you know, opium. You buy some sweet Palestinian chocolate and munch hopefully.

When the lights go off again, it's a snafu for the operator. He runs four technicolor minutes of *Gone With the Wind* before he realizes his mistake. Lights on again. More chocolate and then back to the Marx Brothers.

By this time you are beginning to wonder whether a beer wouldn't have been better. You have been invaded by a number of small animals left on the seat by some earlier visitor. As they deploy unerringly for the more vital parts of your anatomy, you wonder whether you need a shot for typhus.

Scratching with one hand, clinging to the now dissolved

chocolate bar with the other, and totally confused between French captions, Irani cut-ins, and English dialogue, you may as well give up. It's a nice cool ride back to camp in the truck, long enough for sober thought. You resolve to stick to beer and leave the movies to Special Service.

---

★

---

A solider stationed in the South Pacific wrote to his wife in the States to please send him a harmonica to occupy his free time and keep his mind off of the local women. The wife complied and sent the best one she could find, along with several dozen lesson books and sheet music.

Rotated back home, he rushed home and through the front door where his wife was waiting. "Oh darling," he gushed, "Come here. . . . Let me look at you, let me hold you! Let's have a fine dinner out, then make love all night. I've missed your loving so much!"

The wife, keeping her distance, said, "All in good time, lover. First, let's hear you play that harmonica."

---

★

---

From *The Best from* Yank, *the Army Weekly* (Dutton, 1945)

## FURLOUGH GREETINGS
by T.5 James P. Charles

"My, how nice you look in your uniform. Stand over in the light so I can see you better."

"So *you're* what's defending me!"

"You've certainly filled out since you got in the Army. You must get awfully good food."

"You may as well stay home nights while you're here. All the girls are either married or gone off to work in defense plants."

"How come you've been in nine months and only one stripe?"

"Gee, I wish I was in your shoes. They wouldn't take me on account of my eyes."

"You can be a lot of help while you're here. The cook just quit."

"I don't see why you don't write more often, with all the free time you boys have."

"You young fellows are lucky. If I wasn't an old man with a family, I'd volunteer in a minute."

"I don't see why you want to go out with that girl tonight. After all, we haven't seen you in six months."

"Why don't you and your wife spend your first night home with us? We can put you up in the living room on the day bed."

"I saw your old girlfriend out dancing the other night. She was with a lieutenant."

"Why don't you wire your captain for an extension?"

"The Army will be a good thing for you. It'll teach you to obey orders."

"The trouble with this Army is, they're making it too easy on you men. Why, back in '17——"

"Would you like to ride out and take a look at the new Army camp?"

"There's a dance at the USO tonight. Why don't you and Sally go?"

"Did they issue you oars with those shoes?"

"How do you-all like it living down South?"

"Remember that fellow who was trying to cut you out with Mary Lou? He's got a job at the airplane factory."

"Aw, I'll bet one of those Southern belles has got you under her thumb."

"Charlie, dear, can I have your regimental insignia? I'm making a collection from all the boys I know in the Army."

"Gee, I think those fatigue hats are cute."

# ARMY VS. NAVY VS. MARINES VS. AIR FORCE VS. . . .

Two men were bragging about their different platoons. "Why, my outfit is in such good shape—so well drilled," declared one fellow, "that when they present arms all you can hear is slap, slap, click."

"Very good," conceded the other, "but when my company presents arms you just hear slap, slap, jingle."

"What's the jingle?" asked the first.

"Oh," replied the other off-handedly, "just our medals."

---

★

---

Mark passed his enlistment exam easily. The doctor asked, "Why do you want to join the Navy, son?"

"My father told me it'd be a good idea, sir."

"Oh? And what does your father do?"

"He's in the Army, sir."

---

★

---

The Army Airborne major was accustomed to harassment from Air Force fliers about crazy Army paratroopers jumping out of perfectly good aircraft. "Obviously, the Air Force is aware that there's no such thing as a 'perfectly good aircraft,' " the irritated officer finally countered one afternoon, "because they pay you bastards four times as much to stay in one as the Army pays its men to jump."

"Oh, you've got it all wrong, Major," an Air Force sergeant replied. "The Army figures anyone stupid enough to jump out of an airplane voluntarily is gonna be too dumb to bitch about the salary."

---

★

# ACCIDENTAL INSUBORDINATION AND OTHER MISCELLANEOUS OCCURRENCES IN THE LINE OF DUTY

One stormy night, a Marine private was on his first guard duty assignment.

Presently, a general stepped out to take his dog for a walk.

The nervous young private snapped to attention, made a perfect salute, and cried out, "Sir, Good Evening, Sir!"

The general, out for some relaxation, returned the salute and said, "Good evening soldier. Nice night, isn't it?"

It was hardly a nice night, but the private wasn't about to disagree with the general, so he saluted again and replied, "Sir, Yes Sir!"

The general continued, "You know there's something about a stormy night that I find soothing. It's all really relaxing, don't you agree?"

The private didn't agree, but then the private was just a private, and responded "Sir, Yes Sir!"

Indicating the dog, the general said, "This is a Golden Retriever, the best type of dog to train."

The private glanced at the dog, saluted yet again. "Sir, Yes Sir!"

The general continued, "I got this dog for my wife."

The private said, "Good trade, Sir!"

---

Contributed to *Reader's Digest*'s "Humor in Uniform" by Tom Tierney

At the shore base in England where I was stationed during World War II, reasons for reporting back late from leave ranged from the believable to the outrageous. But a prize should have gone to the sailor who, when asked why he had missed his train, stoutly protested, "I did catch the train, sir . . . but it got away," and produced the compartment-door handle as evidence.

---

From *More G.I. Laughs: Real Army Humor*, selected by Harold Hersey (Sheridan House, 1944)

### Army vs. Ant

*The following letter is an actual answer written by an officer in reply to a communication about procurement of insecticide. The names of the persons and outfits involved have been deleted, for obvious reasons.*

"1. Following telephone information from your office that you were unable to issue carbon disulphide for use in this office in ant control, and following receipt of your letter listing insect repellents furnished by your office—request was made of quartermaster for carbon disulphide for use by this office in ant control. We were informed by Quartermaster that they could only issue such preparation if the ant to be exterminated was in the building. If it was outside the building, the issuance of such preparation properly should come from Engineering. It is difficult to determine the intention of the ants we are attempting to exterminate—Some live inside and wander outside for food, while some live outside and forage inside for food. It is rather a difficult problem to determine which ant comes from without and is what you might call an Engineering ant, and which ant comes from within and is what would be a Quartermaster ant. Some of our ants appear to be going in circles and others apparently are wandering at random with no thought of destination— such ant tactics are very confusing and could result in a Quartermaster ant being exterminated by an Engineering poison or an Engineering ant being exterminated by a Quartermaster poison.

"2. In view of the fact that Quartermaster-issued poison has been found to kill the ant just as dead as Engineering-issued poison—and vice versa, request is made that your office draw identical poison for issue to this office from both Engineering and Quartermaster and to mix same so there will be no way of knowing which poison killed the ant—the assumption being that no well-bred G.I. ant would eat other than poison issued through proper channels to final destination—which destination being aforementioned dead or dying ant."

---------------------------------★---------------------------------

"You'll get over it, Joe. Oncet I wuz gonna write a book exposin' the army after th' war myself."

From *The Best from* Yank, *the Army Weekly* (Dutton, 1945)

## NOMENCLATURE OF WHISTLE, M1

by Private Raymond Zauber

*Editor's Note:* This splendid piece of satire describes the simple "air-cooled whistle," but strictly in GI handbook terminology.

The U.S. whistle, model M1, is a self-repeating, shoulder-strap model. It is lung-operated, air-cooled, reverberating-blast type. The whistle weighs an ounce and a half, and the chain another half-ounce.

The whistle is divided into two parts—the whistle-cylinder blowing assembly, and the whistle-retaining chain assembly. At the blowing aperture there are two raised sections, one on each side, called the upper-teeth guard lug and the lower-teeth guard lug, respectively. The remainder of the whistle apparatus is known as the chamber-cylinder operating assembly. This consists of the opening-sound emission slot, the cylinder-butt lock onto which the whistle-retaining chain assembly is attached, and the cylinder-reverberating operating cork.

The whistle-retaining chain consists of the shoulder-strap button-hook catch which secures the whistle for carrying and operation. The shoulder-strap button-hook catch is locked by the upper-chain retaining ring. The chain is also fastened to the lower-chain retaining ring which is looped through the cylinder-butt lock of the whistle cylinder-blowing assembly.

The whistle is carried in the upper left pocket of the blouse or jacket. To use, unbutton or unsnap pocket with fingers of the right hand, remove whistle by raising directly up on retaining chain. When the whistle swings free of the pocket, grasp the sides of the whistle-blowing assembly with the thumb and forefinger of the left hand and with the upper-teeth lug facing up and to the rear. Then place between the center of lips and clamp lips firmly so that no air can escape.

The sound is produced by taking a deep breath through the nostrils and exhaling it through the mouth into the air-compressing blow channel. After the blast return the whistle to the pocket by the reverse of the steps used for removal.

Disassembling of all parts, other than the shoulder-strap button-hook catch and the lower-chain retaining ring, is for ordinance only.

★

From *More G.I. Laughs: Real Army Humor*, selected by Harold Hersey (Sheridan House, 1944)

## Pup Tents Too Cozy

I've always had the feeling that the Army invented the pup tent just to prove to every soldier that battle can be won if all parties cooperate; for believe me, when two jeeps try to crawl into the three-by-six to nest down among gas masks, tin helmets, and poles, even cooperation is subject to a tight squeeze.

Now the ideal method of double-bunking in this tarpaulin hut is not to sleep in it at all, but rather to get engrossed in a crap game which lasts until dawn. But since I was never lucky and my knees are not the housemaid variety, there always comes the time to face the inevitable.

To start with, the pairing of bed mates is stupid, for it always ends up with the two ballooniest jeeps in the outfit matching tarpaulin sheets, and being on the inflated side myself, I invariably get another ten-by-ten partner.

After the tent is pitched and well anchored for the ensuing tussle, we begin. If possible, I manage to be the first of our Arbuckle duo to squash into the canvas tunnel. Then with the assistance of my cohort, I attempt to hoist my avoir du poise over to one side of the tent, but without success.

And so the stage is set for the real struggle. My fellow sheet slinger lies prone and tries to sneak in without being noticed. I cooperate and [snore] more loudly during this procedure, but it just doesn't pan out. No matter how indifferently we may be to the situation, the facts remain the same. Two fat men weren't meant to sleep in the same tent.

At last in desperation, my cohort reaches the grunting stage. He wiggles. He pushes. He curses. He lunges. In the meantime, I try to sleep, for the moment is coming when I won't be able to breathe, much less sleep.

Next morning we pressed hams never attempt to crawl out. It is much simpler to pull stakes without ever getting out of our blankets. After the tent has collapsed and has been tossed aside, both of us can arise and waddle off in our separate directions without interference.

It's not that I object to seeing how the other half lives, but I do wish the Army would issue pup tents in sizes. It would save the wear and tear on my second front.

*"Why th' hell couldn't you have been born a beautiful woman?"*

---

★

---

From *The GI War, 1941–1945,* by Ralph G. Martin (Avon, 1967)

It was a "Dear John" letter in reverse, a girl from Nebraska complaining because her GI was deserting her for an Australian girl. "What has she got that I haven't got?" the American girl wanted to know.

"Nothing," wrote her former boyfriend, "but she's got it here."

---

★

---

Contributed to *Reader's Digest*'s "Humor in Uniform" by Zyg Jelinski

During the War, Polish pilots in Great Britain were famous for showing off their flying skills. One morning I was returning from a flight test and made the mistake of beginning my landing approach at too low a speed. Just as I crossed the airfield, my plane stalled, dropped from 20 feet onto the landing strip and bounced back into the air. I gave it full throttle but the plane leaned onto its left wing, and I was off the runway. In desperation, I cut all power and applied full right brake. The aircraft swung 180 degrees, back onto the landing strip, tail first. The sturdy P-51 was undamaged. "Did you see that plane?" gasped a visiting air commodore. "Not to worry, sir," the RAF commanding officer replied. "It's only one of those crazy Poles trying to show off."

---

★

---

From *More G.I. Laughs: Real Army Humor*, selected by Harold Hersey
(Sheridan House, 1944)

## VISITING HOURS
**There's Nothing to Do but Relapse**
**As Your Pals Make It a Beautiful Morning**
by Private Robert A. Corley

Visiting hours at the station hospital are the bright spot of a patient's day. That's why Pvt. Tim Rushin and I were on our way to visit Kirk—to spread cheer.

Kirk, that's Pvt. Kirk Morrison, broke his finger in the coin return slot of a telephone and was crushed in the folding doors of the booth when he tried to free himself. Tim and I didn't know the full extent of Kirk's injuries, but we did know that he was despondent and feeling lower than a coal mine's deepest pit.

So we were on a mission of mercy. We were on the way to cheer Kirk up, to boost his morale and give him a new outlook on life.

"There's ward A-3," Tim said. We went in and were soon at Kirk's bedside.

"Hello fellas," he croaked weakly.

"Greetings, Gate," we said in a reverent whisper.

"Howya feeling?" asked Tim.

"Can't complain," said Kirk. "What's new?"

"Nothin' new," I said. "How's every little thing?"

"Oh every little thing's all right," he replied. Then he asked, "How're things at the squadron?"

"Things are all right," I told him.

Tim said, "When are you getting out of this joint?"

"Don't know," Kirk told him.

I just stood there wrapped in my thoughts.

"How have you been?" Kirk asked.

My string of thoughts unraveled. "Huh? Oh I've been fair to middling," I answered.

"Yeah," added Tim, "mostly middling. Now me, I've been tolerable well all week."

"How's the food here?" I asked.

"Could be better," was Kirk's terse reply.

"Are you sure you're feeling all right?" asked Tim.

"Yeah, I guess so, why do you ask?"

Before I could stop Tim, he was saying, "Gee, you certainly look bad. I had an uncle who wasn't hurt half as bad as you are now. He just crushed a toe in a threshing machine and he died three days later."

Quickly I tried to counteract Tim's bad taste in mentioning death to Kirk. "Things aren't that bad," I said, "but it wouldn't hurt to draw up a will just in case. The War Department has been urging soldiers to draw up their will so that their estates will go to the right persons." I wasn't sure whether or not I had completely made up for Tim's horrible blunder.

"Are you warm enough?" Tim asked anxiously.

Kirk moaned, "I guess so."

"Gosh, but you're pale," commented Tim. "Your eyes are sorta glassy and sunk back in your head too." Then, clucking his tongue sympathetically, he added, "He could pass for a corpse right now, couldn't he?"

"Well, now that you've mentioned it, yes he could," I agreed.

Kirk gave a low moan.

The nurse came in then to chase us out so we promised Kirk that we would come back real soon and cheer him up again, but we never got back to see him. Right after we left, his condition became critical and no visitors were permitted.

Finally, there came the day when Kirk was permitted to leave the hospital, and Tim and I were right on hand to welcome him as he left the hospital.

"Hi fellas," Kirk called. "Long time no see. Gee it's great to see you again."

"Boy," Tim whistled under his breath, but still much too loud. "He's lost weight. Why that skeleton doesn't look like Kirk at all."

"Kirk," I said, "are you sure you're well? You look worse now than you did when you came to the hospital. You're so thin and frail. I had an aunt once who was emaciated like you are now. She died from tuberculosis. You don't look well at all!"

Kirk crumpled silently to the ground. I started to speak, but Tim nosed me out by a syllable. "Quick," he shouted. "Get a doctor, get a nurse, get the medical corps, get an ambulance, GET SOMETHING!"

Then Tim says to me, "Seems to me they'd take better care of the patients. Can you imagine? It's terrible, I can't understand it, letting Kirk out before he was well."

# ENEMIES
# AND
# FRIENDS

A young man who volunteered for military service during World War II had such a high aptitude for aviation that he was sent right to Pensacola, skipping boot camp altogether.

On the first day at the Pensacola base, he soloed and proved himself to be the best flier on the base. He was immediately issued his gold wings, and assigned to an aircraft carrier in the South Pacific.

On his first day in the Pacific, he took off and single-handedly shot down six Japanese Zeroes. Then, climbing up to 20,000 feet, he located nine more Japanese planes and shot them all down, too.

Noting that his fuel was getting low, he descended, circled the carrier, and came in for a perfect landing on the deck. He threw back the canopy, climbed out of the plane, and jogged over to the captain. Saluting smartly, he said, "Well sir, how did I do on my first day?"

The captain replied, "You make one velly impoltant mistake!"

From *Leading with My Left*, by Richard Armour (New Leader, 1945)

## DIVINITY? FUDGE!

*Hirohito Says He Is Really Not Divine*
 —NEWSPAPER HEADLINE

Please do not bow before me,
Oh, good people, don't adore me!
 Just a nod would be quite fine.
I want no genuflection
Nor low bends in my direction,
 For I'm really not divine.

I don't know how it got started
Or by whom it was imparted,
 But the notion wasn't mine.
It occurred that, rather oddly,
People thought that I was godly,
 Though I'm really not divine.

My great granddad or his pappy
May have been the guilty Jappy
 Who began the sacred line
And somehow got us into
All this mix-up over Shinto,
 Yet *I'm* really not divine.

I'm an ordinary mortal
Who can cry and who can chortle.

To be more, I've no design.
I am friendly and forgiving
And quite happy to be living,
    But I'm *really* not divine!

---- ★ ----

From *The Best from* Yank, *the Army Weekly* (Dutton, 1945)

## THE NEW YORK SUBWAY SYSTEM
## ON THE ITALIAN FRONT
by Sergeant Newton H. Fulbright

WITH THE FIFTH ARMY IN ITALY—Perhaps some busy somebody has taken care of the matter—I haven't been able to read anything much lately—but in case it hasn't been done, I think the New York subway system should receive proper credit for its part in the war here in Italy.

I first came across this curious connection of the venerable and undramatic subway with the war here in Italy one morning shortly after daylight on the beaches of Paestum. I was standing behind an Italian farmhouse a little undecided about things. A German M34 machine gun had been chattering a little while before across a corn patch, and I was supposed to go in that direction. I was sitting there thinking about things when a little Italian farmer came up and started speaking English.

The Germans had gone, he said, up the road they had gone.

"Thanks," I said. "Where did you learn to speak English?"

"I work for the New York subway system five years," he said.

Later in the afternoon a few of us from L Company and M Company plodded up the 3,500-foot slope of Mount Soprano, overlooking the beach. A battery of 88s had rained concentrated hell on us from the mountain since daylight.

Nearing the town of Carpaccio, we slowed up a little. Red communication wire, Jerry's sure trail, led around the mountain, where the forward observer had been, and along the rugged winding road to Carpaccio, where the 88s were supposed to be. We didn't know what was in front of us, so we moved along cautiously.

Then an Italian came out of a farmhouse and told us all about it.

"They've gone—all gone! Run away to the east. They all been drunk all afternoon. They get all *vino* in town, then they run away."

He had worked for the New York subway system five years.

I met a Boston subway worker a night or two later.

Some of us had taken a patrol into Trentinara just to see if there were any Germans in the place. I found myself walking up a main street as dark as deep-land sorghum syrup and as crooked as the stick held by the crooked man who walked a crooked mile in the nursery rhyme; and the place was not only dark, it seemed completely deserted. Our artillery had been shelling the town and the natives had mostly taken to the hills.

I nosed along, followed by a few G.I.s who didn't like the situation and plainly said so. Suddenly an Italian stepped out of a dark alley with outstretched hand and said, "Hello."

We had quite a conversation there in the dark street. Other Italians crept out of hiding timidly, and presently there was a small crowd of us talking and laughing.

The Germans had all gone. They had left the day before, 18 of them, dressed in civilian clothes.

"They throw away their guns, they go northeast," one man said, pointing to a mountain. Tall and wistful and white in the daytime, it reminded me somehow of the Chrysler Building in New York. "No more Germans left in this whole country. The shepherds come in from the hills and report all Germans fleeing," he said.

He wanted to talk more about Boston (he had helped build the Boston subway) and Brookline and all those Back Bay places.

Some days later when I managed to escape from the Germans about 100 miles behind their lines, I had the courage to stop at an Italian farmhouse largely because I remembered these incidents and the New York subway system.

I had been captured with five of my men while on reconnaissance behind enemy lines on September 14 at the bloody battle of Altaville. Five days later, I made my escape and started back in the night toward our lines, far to the south.

Jerry was all over the country but principally on the highways, trying to withdraw his tremendous, ponderous equipment to new positions north of the Volturno River. I stumbled across country, dodging villages and dogs. Dogs sailed out every so often, yelping and howling. The moon was down; I was glad for that, and yet it was a hindrance. I was always bumping into things. Once I suddenly discovered I was walking down the principal street of a village, but I was able to back out of the place without being discovered.

After a few of these mishaps, I decided to travel by day.

I picked out a nice-looking farmhouse, a couple of miles west of a village, and crawled into a straw stack to wait for morning.

The old lady who saw me first was scared out of her wits. She dashed for the doorway while I stood in the yard trying to smile and wiping wheat straw out of my beard.

In the farmhouse I discovered that no one could speak English. The farmer couldn't, his wife couldn't, his mother couldn't, his sister couldn't, and neither could his three little daughters or a boy whose mother was dead.

I'd say something in Spanish or English or a mixture of both, and they'd just shake their heads and laugh. I would shake hands with everyone again, point at myself, and say like a bright Fuller Brush man: "*Americano!* Me *Americano! Americano* and *Italiano* (stepping hard on the ano) friends! Good! *Bueno!*"

Suddenly someone entered the door.

I turned and faced a bulky, heavy-set Italian with a red, important-looking face, who held a pistol within a few inches of my stomach.

This should have been serious. Yet I wanted to laugh. The pistol was so small it looked like a cap pistol, and it was so completely covered with rust that I doubted whether it would fire at all. I stood there while the heavy fellow went through my trouser pockets. He hauled out the few items I possessed: a broken pencil, a fountain pen, a notebook, a billfold containing three genuine American gold-seal 10-dollar bills, and a picture of my girl.

After that he sat down on a little stool and put the pistol in his hip pocket. He didn't seem to know just what else to do.

Then an old Italian with proud, graying moustache entered the door.

"Gooda de mornin'!"

"Good morning!" I shouted. I jumped up and grabbed him by the arm and started shaking hands as though I were an Elk meeting a fellow Elk in Amarillo. "But where in hell did you learn to speak English?"

"I work seventeen years for the New York subway system," he said. And from that moment on I was a firm believer in the New York subway.

We sat down and talked a long time. I got rid of my G.I. clothes and got into a ragged civilian shirt and trousers. I felt like going out and grabbing a hoe and going to work on the farm right away.

That night the mayor of the town and other influential Italians called on me.

One of them, a miller, pulled a yellowed sheet of paper out of his pocket and showed me an honorary discharge from the United States Army, dated 1918.

"I lived in New York before the war," he said. "I was a doorman for the New York subway system."

He opened his mouth and started shouting the names of the stations—Spring, Canal, 14th, 34th, 42nd. After that, he sang songs that had been popular during the last war: "Oh, How I Hate To Get Up In The Morning" and "Are You From Dixie?" I remember my aunt singing that one years ago.

I hid in the farmhouse for five days. Meanwhile the British Eighth Army was driving up rapidly from the south. When the flash of artillery could be seen plainly in the mountains and when the rumble sounded loud like spring thunder in Texas, I headed out for the wars again.

It was tough going; I was 16 days getting inside our lines. And—well, there were other former employees of the New York and Boston subway systems along the road, or I probably wouldn't have made it.

So my hat is off to the New York subway system. Viva the New York subway system, a great institution!

★

After seeing to it that Italy's trains ran on time, Mussolini was feeling proud enough to order the government printing office to issue a stamp featuring his likeness. Much to his dismay, however, postal workers began complaining that the stamps were falling off envelopes. Every day, layers of the stamps filled the bottoms of their carrier bags.

*"When I think of all the time I spent in basic*

Mussolini rushed to the printer and demanded to know why the highest grade of glue hadn't been used on his stamps. "But it was, *il Duce*!" the horrified manager insisted. "We've looked into this unfortunate situation, and the problem is that people are spitting on the wrong side!"

---

★

---

A group of Polish soldiers was briefed by their captain just before the blitzkrieg.

"Men, as you know, ammunition is in short supply. Thus, we must ask this question: If you were confronted by a German soldier and a Russian soldier, which one would you shoot?"

Sheepish Private Lutovsky answered, "The German, sir."

*raining creeping and crawling it makes me sick."*

"Really? And why?"

"Business before pleasure, sir."

---

★

---

As World War II began, the highly superstitious Hitler asked his astrologer to come up with a chart that would predict the war's outcome.

"We don't need a chart for that," the astrologer said. "Just a coin."

"A coin?" asked Hitler.

"Yes. Flip a coin. If it lands heads up, then Germany will win. If it lands tails up, Great Britain will be victorious."

"And if," Hitler hedged, "it lands on its edge?"

"In that case," the astrologer said, "it's a miracle, and Poland will win."

---

★

---

After Mussolini died, St. Peter made a special visit to hell to make sure that certain sinners were receiving adequate punishment. Eventually, he came upon Hitler, who was standing in feces up to his chin—and smiling.

"I don't understand," St. Peter declared. "How can you smile when you know you'll be spending all of eternity in excrement?"

"I'm smiling," Hitler replied, "because I'm standing on Mussolini's shoulders."

---

★

---

# SECRET WEAPONS FOR THE INVASION OF GERMANY

## By Sgt. RALPH STEIN

**OLD TOWN INVASION BARGE, SUBMERSIBLE, MARK VII, SECTION 8 (WITH PARASOL AND BANJO)**

OUR simple-hearted Nazi coast sentry thinks that he sees only romantic couples, spending Sunday afternoon in canoes. But beneath the surface our invading troops are lurking, well supplied with Spam for the fight that looms ahead and studying their comic books as the Zero Hour draws near. TECHNICAL DATA: Notice the young lady, or frail, in the stern of the canoe. She steers the barge with that innocent hand which she trails so languidly in the water and conceals with her distracting legs, or hockeys, the trap door in the floor of the canoe which serves the attacking force as an exit from the barge.

**TRACTION REDUCER, BOOT M13, OR PRATT-FALL INDUCER**

THIS two-man motorized dignity destroyer features a pair of automatic hands which pick bananas very rapidly, dropping the peels in the path of advancing enemy infantry. Rest of the banana goes into GI pudding which is used as a devastating booby trap. Automatic hands can also be used to snap fingers under the noses of enemy officers and make other insulting gestures.

HERE is our secret bottle weapon which is used to float troops in battle equipment to Germany by the Gulf Stream, if it happens to be going that way.

## KNACKWURST AND SAUERKRAUT PROJECTOR, OLFACTORY

TRACTOR at left carries an engine-driven fan which forces the odor of knackwurst and sauerkraut, cooking on gas range, through the projector tube. Drool sergeant at projector controls can elevate or depress tube through an arc of 70 degrees. Drool meter under Nazi's chin registers excitation of salivary gland. If victim doesn't drool enough, put some more kraut in the pot. METHOD OF USE: The enemy follows the smell of the knackwurst and kraut and he is yours. Then you don't let him eat it.

### WENCH MORTAR

THESE weapons create confusion by dropping tasty babes or reasonably exact facsimiles upon installations. SERVICE OF THE PIECE: Tube should be swabbed often with perfume, preferably Chanel No. 5.

### PARACOOK, PTOMAINE

THIS cruel weapon of invasion is used only under extreme provocation. Cooks and accomplices armed with copies of the "Army Cook's Field Manual" are dropped behind the enemy's line to cook for him. No special training necessary. Supplies of dried eggs and creamed beef on toast may also be dropped but only as a desperate last resort.

### INCENDIARY, PEDAL M1922 OR HOT FOOT

THIS is a light, mobile, single-seat infantry co-operation weapon, which can also be used to illuminate GI crap games at night when the invasion is over. METHOD OF OPERATION: The bewildered Nazi is chased until exhaustion. Then the embracing ring, or hugger, clamps over his head, pinning his arms to his side while the automatic hand appears with a lighted match, applying a hot foot in the customary manner. When a storm trooper or OBERFELDWEBEL is bagged, the weapon applies the blowtorch with satisfactory results. How do the matches get stuck in the boots of the Nazis? They are placed there weeks before the invasion by fifth-columnists disguised as poor but honest shoe-shine boys.

From *Leading with My Left*, by Richard Armour (New Leader, 1945)

## END MEN

*Adolf Hitler grimly told the German people that "in this war there will be no victors or losers but merely survivors and annihilated."*

—NEWS ITEM

It may be, Adolf, may well be,
    As you've so grimly stated,
One side will be survivors, and
    One side annihilated.

But now you've told us what is what,
    We'll tell you who is who:
Survivors, Adolf, that is us,
    Annihilated, you!

## BRIEF CASE

*Hitler is reported to have developed a phobia of briefcases since the attempt upon his life*                    —NEWS ITEM

Gestapo chiefs and diplomats
    Who come to see the Fuehrer,
Please check your briefcase with your hats,
    And he will feel securer.
For who can tell what lurks therein
    Of bomb, grenade, or hatchet,
What searing acid, strong as sin,
    With which he's sure to catch it.

There may, indeed be close to reach
    Some secret weapons medley—
Or typescript of a Goebbels speech,
    Which would be far more deadly.

## DEAD LEVEL

*Rumored Hitler Made Last Stand Beneath Berlin Zoo*
                              —NEWSPAPER HEADLINE

Among the rumors freely penned
    Comes one I hope is true:
They say that Hitler met his end
    Beneath the Berlin Zoo.
It's just the sort of proof one needs
    That justice has not ceased:
It means his death was, like his deeds,
    A bit below the beast.

# CELEBRITIES

From the foreword to *Always Home*, the USO's pictorial history of its first fifty years, quoted in *Over Here, Over There*, by Maxene Andrews and Bill Gilbert (Zebra Books, 1993)

Bob Hope wrote: "Thanks to the USO, my knowledge of geography has been greatly enhanced. And I have some wonderful memories—like box lunches, yellow fever shots—and I've learned how to say Kaopectate in nine languages.... I knew the plane was old when I saw the pilot sitting behind me wearing goggles and a scarf. [The plane] belonged to a four-star general—Pershing."

--------------------★--------------------

From *I Was There*, by Bob Hope (Bob Hope Enterprises, 1994)

My love for the GI started in 1941—May 6, to be exact. We had just finished a script session for my radio show when I was approached by my producer Al Capstaff in the parking lot. He asked, "How would you like to do a radio show for the military at March Field in Riverside?"

"Invite them to the studio," I offered.

"Too many!" he said.

"How many?" I asked.

"Two thousand."

I blinked—I could hear the sound that two thousand joke-hungry servicemen could make—all laughing and applauding. This was an offer I couldn't resist.

What an audience it was. The show was produced in our established radio format with opening monologue, cast-member comedy, music, a guest star sketch, and the usual commercials. The new difference was the adaptation of our comedy to a military context:

> "How do you do, ladies and gentlemen, this is Bob—March Field—Hope. . . . telling all you soldiers that have to shoot in swamp or march in the brush, if they use Pepsodent no one will ever have to drill in your mush. . . . Well, here we are at March Field, one of the Army's great flying fields, located near Riverside, California, and I want to tell you that I'm thrilled being here . . . and what a wonderful welcome you gave me . . . as soon as I got in the camp, I received a ten-gun salute . . . or so they told me on the operating table. . . . These guys were glad to see me . . . one rookie came running up to me and said, 'Are you really Bob Hope?' I said, 'Yes!' . . . they grabbed his rifle just in time."

My writers had a ball. There was hardly a subject we wouldn't approach.

> "I've just arrived from the States. You know, that's where
> Churchill lives. He doesn't exactly live there, he just goes back
> to deliver Mrs. Roosevelt's laundry."

In Tunis:

> "Hiya, fellow tourists. . . . Well, I'm very happy to be here. But
> of course, I'm leaving as soon as I finish the show. . . . But this
> is a great country . . . Africa . . . this is Texas with Arabs."

And, as so frequently happened, it was a GI who provided
the biggest laugh. . . . Just as I stepped up to the microphone
to start the show, a light tank came shoving through the
crowd like a fat man making for a seat in a crowded subway
car. People gave way in all directions. A tank commands
plenty of respect. I thought it was out of control. It looked
as if the thing was going to mow me down and I was getting
ready to jump off the platform when suddenly, right in front
of me, it stopped.

The top flew open and a guy crawled out wearing a tanker's
crash helmet and grease on his face. He was dragging a folding
chair, which he set up on top of the tank. He sat down, crossed
his legs, smiled, waved at me, and said, "Make me laugh."

Laughs came from simple harebrained foolishness, reluctant
heroism, and even blatant cowardice set against a climate of
high seriousness. We made a point of researching the military lingo and commanding officers' names. The stern military regime evoked laughs, so did the soldiers' resentments,
hardships, and habits. They laughed at me but, most of all,
they laughed at themselves.

On May 20, I took guest star Priscilla Lane and the cast to the San Diego Naval Station. (Sailors like to laugh, too.) And the following week we did a show for the Marines at San Luis Obispo. And on June 10, Mary Martin came with me to the Army's Camp Callan. I was off and running and enjoying every minute spent entertaining the men and women in uniform.

---★---

From *Over Here, Over There: The Andrews Sisters and the USO Stars in World War II*, by Maxene Andrews and Bill Gilbert (Zebra Books, 1993)

Entertainers were being recruited for every kind of personal appearance imaginable. LaVerne, Patty, and I were visiting camps and military hospitals in every city where we played, and other entertainers were doing the same. One of our hospital visits became something of a sentimental journey. It happened back home in Minneapolis when we were visiting the Snelling Veterans Hospital. All three of us were touched when some veterans of World War I and even a few of the Spanish-American War remembered that I sang for them when I was only four years old.

It made me think, not entirely with joy, that I might be one of the few entertainers of my generation who had sung for veterans of America's wars as far back as 1898. For all I know, there could have been some veterans of the Civil War who were residents in that hospital when I sang there as a toddler in the early 1920s. However, I deny emphatically that there is any reason to believe I ever performed for veterans of the Revolutionary War!

. . . Every time we visited the GIs, it did as much for our morale as it did for theirs. . . . Every contact we had with our servicemen and women convinced us about the quality of our people in uniform. They showed us every courtesy, and they never tried to make advances to any of us. We were never considered sex symbols anyhow. We had the girl-next-door image, and that suited us just fine. When we were beginning to sing around Minneapolis at the start of the 1930s, our mother told us, choosing her words the way only a mother can: "Never let it bother you that you're not beautiful. You all have"—then she'd pause—"*wonderful* personalities." With that kind of diplomacy, she could have been Roosevelt's Secretary of State.

Groucho Marx seemed to agree with Mama about our "beauty." We were traveling on the same train with Groucho when he told one of the members of his group: "I thought they made all their trips by broom."

. . . Lou Wills may have been the youngest of the USO entertainers. He was only fourteen when the war started, but already he was performing on stage and in a Broadway show as a comedy dancer and acrobat.

. . . One [of Lou's troupes] included a performer with the stage name of Lord Buckley, who used to pick six GIs out of the audience, stand behind them on stage, and tell them to move their mouths when he tapped them without speaking any words. Then he told the audience that he was going to do the talking for all six of them.

The GIs would be standing there looking as if they were having an enjoyable conversation, but they weren't saying a word. From behind, Lord Buckley was speaking in six voices— different in every way—as the audience collapsed in laughter.

Those USO weekends were a learning experience for Lou XX, and Lord Buckley was the source of one of Lou's early lessons. On a bus ride to a weekend military stop, Lou smelled something strange. He asked the passenger in the seat next to him what that funny smell was.

"Don't you know?"

"No. What is it?"

"Marijuana."

"Lord Buckley would sit in the back of the bus on our way from the airport and smoke pot," Lou says, "and start to preach and chant, 'The Lord sent me down here. He told me that if we all smoke the same thing we'll be flying high and we can fly over this war and we'll all be happy.' He was hilarious, especially with that pot in him."

When his skin began breaking out with large red bumps, Lou went to the family doctor in Yonkers and learned something else—he was allergic to the smoke from Lord Buckley.

. . . Applause and laughter were never so loud, or so easy to get, as when you were playing before GI audiences. They wrote a gag into the routine for that troupe in which Jinx Falkenburg would ask the Ritz Brothers, "Hey—can one of you tell me where a girl can get a date around here?"

Bedlam followed—every time. The guys would jump out of their chairs or up off the ground and holler up to the stage, "Hey, Jinx! Here I am! Over here!"

One of the Ritz Brothers would ask her, "Jinx, look at all those faces. How do they make you feel?"

Jinx: "Like Little Red Riding Hood."

Ritz Brother: "Yeah, they *do* look like a pack of wolves, don't they?"

"It didn't make any difference what you said," Jinx said later.

That's how appreciative the GI audiences were—and it was also how anxious all of us were to laugh.

. . . Even my little dog, Tyrone, discovered how to get an easy laugh during the war. . . . [One night] Tyrone got tired of waiting [offstage], or of our act, and walked onto the stage. After we finished our number and before we went into our next one, the three of us just stood there looking at him—and he sat there, head cocked and tail wagging, looking at us.

Finally, Patty put her hands on her hips and said to Tyrone for the first time in his life, "Now what would you do if *Der Fuehrer* walked in here right now?"

That little thing got right up from where he was sitting in the middle of the stage, walked to the front, straight to the floor microphone, lifted his leg, and wet the base of the mike. The applause was deafening.

---

★

From *Take My Wife . . . Please! The Autobiography of Henny Youngman*
(Berkeley Medallion, 1973)

I guess the most vivid memory I have of playing a military base with Kate [Smith] was when we went to Catalina Island off the coast of Southern California. I made the trip with a mezuzah in one hand and a crucifix in the other. The Catholics were so scared they were telling their beads, and I was so scared I was telling the Catholics to put in a good word for me. The reason for all this fright was that the waters all around Catalina Island were mined. That was because the island had so many antiaircraft guns on it that if they were all fired at once, the recoil would have pushed the island right down to the bottom of the Pacific.

We made it safely, but [the show had to be cancelled due to the death of President Roosevelt]. We ... went back home through the minefields. But this time we didn't make it. Ladies and gentlemen, this whole book is a recording.

---

★

---

From *The Friars Club Encyclopedia of Jokes* (Black Dog & Leventhal/Workman, 1997)

The great comedian Buddy Hackett remembers, "We had a colonel named Fat Ass Johnson. That wasn't his real name, but they called him Fat Ass Johnson. No one ever called him Fat Ass Johnson to his face, but I once called him that on the phone. You see, I was working in the motor pool. That's where they keep trucks and jeeps and vehicles like that.

"The phone rings. The sign said, 'Recruits, do not answer phone.' I didn't know what's a recruit, so I said hello.

"A voice said, 'Soldier, what vehicles have you got available?'

"I said, 'Six trucks, seven jeeps, an MA armored car, a half-track, and Fat Ass Johnson's command car.'

"He said, 'Have you any idea who you're talking to?'

"I said, 'No, sir.'

"He said, 'This is Colonel Johnson.'

"I said, 'Colonel, do you have any idea who you're talking to?'

"He said, 'No.'

"I said, 'Bye-bye, Fat Ass!' "

---

★

---

From *The GI War, 1941–1945*, by Ralph G. Martin (Avon, 1967)

[At an outdoor show for the troops in Naples] a few soldiers spotted Humphrey Bogart, and walked over quickly. One of the guys kidded him about his movie *Sahara*. "Where in the hell did you ever get a .45-caliber pistol that could fire sixteen shots without reloading, Mr. Bogart?" Or, "How come you crossed the whole desert without refilling your gas tank?"

Bogart smiled. "Hollywood is a wonderful place," he said. "They can do anything."

Bogart listened to the loud cheering being given to his second show of that day, and said, "There's nothing very fancy about our show.... Just some singing and skits and gags, but the boys all seem to like it. Especially those guys in the hospital. I guess that's because it makes them forget for a few minutes those shrapnel holes or that missing leg. I've never heard any of those guys bitch or gripe about anything yet. If they have the strength to smile, they smile. It makes a guy proud."

Bogart was quiet for a while, and then he smiled faintly and rubbed a black welt over his right eye. "I was almost in the hospital myself," he said. "I celebrated my forty-fourth birthday a few weeks ago, and I had a bunch of the boys over for a few drinks. Well, we had bum cognac and worse vino, and before I knew it, I was on the table with a paratrooper, and we were yelling 'Geronimo' and jumping off...."

Bogart rubbed his eye again. "I guess my chute failed to open," he said, laughing.

His wife was just finished singing "Stardust," and Bogart flicked away his cigarette and coughed again and said, "That's my cue again," and he hopped up on the side of the truck, stepped in front of the mike and put on his movie-tough face and said, "I'm looking for a new mob.... You guys look like a likely bunch of triggermen...."

Everybody laughed again.

------------------------------------★------------------------------------

When the taciturn British novelist Evelyn Waugh returned from Crete in 1941, he was asked about his impression of the first battle he had ever witnessed. "Like German opera," he replied, "too long and too loud."

------------------------------------★------------------------------------

American humorist and playwright George S. Kaufman remarked on the German strategy behind the invasion of Russia: "I think from now on they're shooting without a script."

------------------------------------★------------------------------------

From *The Best from* Yank, *the Army Weekly* (Dutton, 1945)

## INVASION OF MAE WEST'S DRESSING ROOM
by Sergeant Al Hine

Bob Schwartz Y2c, Yank's sailor, and I arrived a little early at the theater for our date with Mae West. We had to wait ten minutes in a backstage passage before the great lady, who is playing the Empress of All the Russias in a tailored turkey called *Catherine Was Great*, could see us.

Mr. Rosen, Miss West's manager, came out to tell us she would be ready in a minute. A little blonde girl who had already changed her costume hit Mr. Rosen for five dollars. "This is a very expensive place for me to stand," said Mr. Rosen.

Everyone stared at Schwartz's uniform and at my uniform; they were both so drab next to those of the stage Russians who were passing by.

After we'd waited some more, Mr. Rosen finally showed us into her dressing room. Directly in front of the door was a washstand with a friendly but empty Piel's beer bottle under it. To the right was Miss West in a flowing robe and a headdress trimmed with gold sequins, with red-rimmed spectacles in her left hand and a diamond ring on her right-hand third finger. The ring was composed of six or four ice cubes. It was large and heavy enough to fell a kulak or a prime minister at one blow. We could see that "Catherine Was Great" indeed.

Unhappily to report, we couldn't see much more. Miss West's famous frontpiece was in evidence but chastely shielded. She kept switching the skirts of her dressing table over her lap as if she were ashamed of her legs. The sailor and I asked her odds and ends of questions, and she answered them in a very good humor.

"I created this Di'mond Lil character so well," she said, chewing vigorously on her gum and slurring her speech in the manner that has made her famous, "that I was gettin' so I was typed. That's why I figgered on doin' somethin' in a little different line. I bet you boys really thought I was that kinda woman—Di'mond Lil-like—di'nt you? Bet you thought when you came in I'd just throw it at you?" She laughed a little, and then we laughed a little at the very thought of anyone having such a ridiculous impression.

"First idea I had, a long time back, before I went to Hollywood, was doin' a play on the Queena Sheba. When I got around to it, I figgered that it was maybe too Biblical—might make trouble. So I took a look at history just to see what other queens there was around. That's how I found Catherine.

"Wunnerful character, Catherine. Great woman. She had a real bad streak in her a little like my Di'mond Lil. But mighty smart.

"Know why she was so smart?" Miss West snapped this one out like a school teacher. We stammered, "No."

"Smart because she had so many lovers," Miss West said triumphantly. "Mostly a woman just has one man. She gets to know everything he knows, but that's not much. Now my Catherine, she had 300 lovers. Started out when she was 11 years old. That's a lotta men, and she got inside their minds, too.

"These pillow conversations," Miss West purred. "You learn a lotta stuff that way."

The sailor asked her how she felt about the criticisms of her show; it had been panned unanimously by the first-night wolf pack, but it was still playing to full houses with standees.

"I never read 'em," said Miss West. "I'm constructive kinda person. Don't believe in readin' destructive kinda trash. The way I figger is those critics came up against a play that was so fine, so sincere, so puhfick they knew there wasn't anything they could write in praise would add to it. So they went off and panned it. See what I mean? That's kinda people critics are."

Mr. Rosen popped his head in the door and reminded her that there was a rehearsal of a tricky part of the last act coming up. Mae shooed him away. "They still got all that stuff before I come on to rehearse," she said. "After I come on it goes smooth anyway."

"Do you have many servicemen in your audiences, Miss West?" I asked. "Do GIs write you fan letters? What do they write about?"

"Always servicemen," Miss West said, "and thousands of letters from servicemen. You know what they write about? You know what they want to know?"

As I shook my head she removed the gum she had been working on throughout the interview.

"They wanta know if I wear padding," said Miss West. "Hah!" and she patted herself delicately about the prow.

Mr. Rosen popped his head in again, more urgent. Yeoman Schwartz and I rose to leave.

"Come back any time," Miss West said. "Here, I'll give you a pitcha. When they took this we di'n't have a throne or anything on the stage so the bottom part isn't so hot. I'll give you this half." She tore the lower section off a large glossy print and gave it to us. "That's what I look like," she said.

We went out into the alley past the autograph seekers clutching our scrap reverently.

# LOOKING AHEAD

From *Artie Greengroin, Pfc.*, by Harry Brown (Knopf, 1945)

## Artie the Postwar Planner

I was taking a little drive with Artie, who was delivering a few odd tins of Spam to a fairly isolated airfield. We went through country I had never seen before; and I didn't see much of it even then, because of the British penchant for putting high walls and hedges along both sides of the road.

"You're strangely silent, old boy," I said.

Pensive ole Artie nodded his head. "Yerse," he said. "I been thinking of the postwar woild."

"So soon?" I said.

"Yerse," Artie said again. "I decided this war ain't going to hang on more than four or five more years, so I thought I ought to consider the kine of woild that would be waiting to greet Greengroin the Civilian."

"A good idea," I said.

"Sometimes I think it'll look rosy," Artie said, "and sometimes the idea of it gives me the shudders along me spine. Honest to gaw, I can't make up me mine about it."

"I suppose you've made up your mind about the kind of world you want," I said.

"I ain't had much time," Artie said. "The Army's awways after you to think, but they never give you time to think. They's awways some ole bassar of a sergeant standing around ready to innerupt your mental process. But I got a pretty good idea, ole cock, I got a pretty good idea. For one thing, they ain't going to be a Army in the postwar woild, drafted or otherwise."

"Other people have other ideas on that subject."

"Poop on other people," said Artie. "If they ain't careful there won't be no other people in the postwar woild."

"Do you expect to get your old job back?"

"It beats me," Artie said. "I'll be a older man, dignified and poised. I can't waste me life sitting behine the wheel of a hoise. Maybe I'll be capting of industry, a tycoon of fortune."

"Where'll you get your original capital?"

"From craps games," said Artie. "They's lots of money to be picked up in craps games."

"You don't seem to have picked up any of it."

"A run of bad luck," said Artie. "It can't lass."

"It's lasted two years," I said.

Artie shrugged. "I had longer," he said. "For gaw's sake, by the time this war is over I'll be winning millions."

"At least," I said.

"But to get back to the subjeck in question," said Artie, "I'm definaly in favor of the postwar woild. I'm prepared to welcome it with open arms. I been in the Army so long I forgot what a civilian does with his time."

"You've led a very quiet life in the Army."

"Thass the pernt," Artie said. "It's the quiet life that kills a man. If I was fighting a battle or so every other day, I might have a different prospective on things. As it is, I'm disinnerested. The postwar world had better be a awful nice placer or I'm going to be a awful disappernted guy."

"It probably will be," I said.

"It will be a event," said Artie, "to be able to sit down and watch a boid in a tree without some lousy corporal dragging you off to the mess-hall. Did I ever tell you I was a nature fan?"

"I believe you mentioned it," I said.

"I'm a fiend for nature," said Artie. "All the time I used to hang around Prospeck Park in the olden days. And what did it get me? What did me little feathered friends ever do for me? Did they keep me out of the Army? Naw, they didn't keep me out of the Army. If I'd of been borned with no legs and six ears, it wouldn't have kept me out of the Army."

"After the war you can look back at all this and laugh," I said.

"I'll kill myself," said Artie. "I'll giggle meself to death. It'll be a very funny joke. Gaw knows how many years gone out of my life, and I should cry about it. Affer the war I ain't going to do nothing but lap up the lagers and cry in me beer. Thass if there is any beer affer the war."

"You think that there may be no beer?" I asked.

"I ain't saying," said Artie. "But don't be surprised if in the postwar woild there ain't nothing but capsules. And if you think ole Artie is going to walk up to a bar and say: 'Gimme a beer capsule,' you got another think coming. I'll trun myself off a cliff before I reach that state."

"It won't be that bad," I said.

"I don't know," Artie said. "Science has got some gawdam doity tricks up its sleeve. I read a article about it."

"Where?" I asked.

"I don't' remember," Artie said. "In a book. And another thing, they's going to be nothing but airplanes everywheres. And suppose I don't want to loin to fly. People will say: 'There goes Greengroin, the back number. There goes Greengroin, the ole liver in the pass.' What'll happing to me pride? What'll happing to me poise? That'll be a criminal blow."

"After the war driving a plane will be like driving a car," I said.

"I know," said Artie. "Oney there won't be so much traffic. I read all about it. But I ain't innerested. The postwar woild of A. Greengroin is going to consist of steak and beer and clam bakes. They try pulling any of this capsule stuff on ole Artie, they'll get a hit in the head. I read in the papers that they invented a artificial meat out of mush. Thass what theyre trying to do to the woild."

"Whatever it is, it'll be better than the world of the moment," I said.

Artie snorted. "It'll be better because all the sodjers will be civilians again. I don't see nothing else in its favor. They're trying to make a Buck Rogers out of me, thass what they're trying to do. I ain't going to put up with it."

"Hear, hear," I said.

"I came in this war honessly," said Artie. "I didn't ast no

favors of the Army and the Army didn't ast none of me, except to borrow me soul for a few years. But I'm going out of the Army with me eyes wide open. A man's got a right to live his own life."

"Don't forget human progress, old boy," I said.

"I never do," said Artie. "All I'm saying is that I got a dubious streak about the woild affer the war. I don't think I'm going to like it."

"I suppose you'll give it a try, though," I said.

Artie thought for a moment. "Well," he said, "I'll try it out for a couple of days. I'll have me a steak and a couple of beers and then maybe I'll look around and see what shape things is in. If I like them, O.K. But if I don't, I'm going to be a awful mad guy. I'll pull the gawdam walls down, thass what I'll do."

---

★

---

From *More G.I. Laughs: Real Army Humor*, selected by Harold Hersey
(Sheridan House, 1944)

*Editor's Note:* This remarkable parody/meditation originally appeared in the U.S. Army Camp Publication, *The War Doctor.*

## THE CRAVEN

Once upon a midnight dreary, while I pondered, weakly
  bleary
Over what the medics suffer in this cockeyed Total War,
While I brooded, loudly groaning, suddenly there came
  intoning,

A faint sound of someone moaning—moaning at my canvas
  door,
" 'Tis some incubus," I muttered, "moaning at my canvas
  door—
        Only this and nothing more."

Ah, quite clearly I remember, it was in a hot September
And each searing, drying gust whirled in and roughly,
  toughly tore
At the flap upon my tenting. And how vainly I sought—
  panting,
From my rage surcease by ranting—wanting for my chosen
  Lore—
Longing for the lost forgotten talent of the healing Lore—
        Useless here for evermore.

And the harshly rough uncertain rustling of the canvas
  curtain
Chilled me, filled me, with foresighted terrors never known
  before;
So that now, to still the beating of my heart, I lay
  repeating,
" 'Tis some Incubus now reeking damage of our ancient
  Lore;
        Only this, and nothing more."

Presently my heart grew stronger, palpitating then no longer,
"Sir," said I, "or madam, truly your full temperance I
  implore;
The fact is you caught us napping, so quietly you came
  tapping,

As you sneakingly came rapping, sapping at our ancient,
   Lore,
That we scarce were sure we felt you." Here I opened wide
   the door—
       Blackness there and nothing more.


Deep into that blackness peering, long I stood there,
   pondering, fearing,
Doubting, thinking thoughts that medics had no cause to
   think before;
But the silence, though unbroken, still gave back the
   fearful token,
And the only note there spoken was the death knell of our
   Lore.
This I whispered, and an echo murmured, "Dying is your
   lore."
       Merely this and nothing more.


Back into my quarters turning, all my soul within me
   burning,
Soon again I heard a scratching, something louder than
   before,
"Surely," said I, "surely this is something evil to our service;
Let me see, then, what the threat is, and this evil thing
   explore;
Let my dread be stilled a moment and this threat to us
   deplore.
       'Tis the times, and nothing more."


Open then I flung my tent flap, when, with many a burst of
   clap-trap,

In there sneaked a lowly Craven of the faint-heart days
    before.
Not the least obeisance made he; not an instant stopped or
    stayed he;
But when mien, corrupt and shady, perched above my
    canvas door,
Perched above Hippocrates whom we so deeply loved of
    yore.
        Craven, poison, to the core.


Then this vicious bird sat clowning while I sadly kept on
    frowning,
At the greed and lack of ethics on the countenance it wore.
"Though thy aim be black as raven, thou," I said, "is there
    no haven
From your ghastly regimentation of our ancient noble
    Lore?
Tell me what shall be our future at the ending of the war."
        "Writing memos, nothing more."


Much I marveled this ungainly fowl to hear discourse so
    plainly,
Though its clairvoyance no meaning, little relevancy bore;
For who can keep foreseeing that no living human being
Ever will be blessed by seeing medicine in chains; what's
    more
Once bureaucracy begins to rot it quickly at the core,
        Art is gone for evermore.


While the Craven, sitting smirking on that placid bust, is
    working

For one thing: for greedy politics to open wide the door
Nothing further does he utter and no other creed does
    mutter,
So I then could only stutter, "Other fads have gone before;
On the morrow this will leave us, as our fears have flown
    before."
        Then the echo, "Nevermore."


Startled by the stillness broken by reply so aptly spoken,
"Doubtless," said I, "what it utters is its only stock and
    store,
Caught from some unholy master, whom depression and
    disaster
Followed fast and followed faster, till his songs one burden
    bore,
Till the dirges on his fate one melancholy answer bore,
        "Free physicians? Nevermore!"


Then, methought, the air grew denser, stinking of an
    unseen censor
Flushed with power, whose footfalls trampled, stamped
    upon the barren floor.
"Wretch," I cried, "thy vote hath hoaxed thee, thine
    indifference hath coaxed thee,
Respite, respite, and nepenthe from these memories of Lore!
Quaff, nor scoff, this kind nepenthe, but forget your
    healing Lore!"
        Shrieked the Craven, "Nevermore!"


"Prophet!" said I, "Thing of evil—prophet still, if crow or
    devil!

Whether tempter sent or what depression tossed ye here
ashore,
Desolate, no hope implanted, on this desert land
enchanted,
In this trap by war remanded—tell me truly, I implore—
Is there balm for Aesculapiads from this thing we all
implore?"
Quoth the Craven, "Nevermore."

And the Craven, never flitting, still is sitting, still is sitting,
On Hippocrates' pale bust that's just above my quarters'
door;
And his eyes have all the scheming of a demon that is
dreaming;
And the moonlight o'er him streaming throws the shadow
on the floor;
Cast a shadow of the horror soon to come athwart the
moor.
Private practice? NEVERMORE!

──────────────── ★ ────────────────

## THE ARK LANDS ON GUAM
by Corporal Bill Monks

The occupation of Chichi Jima after WWII had come to a
close; we were finally ordered to return to Guam. We had
sent all Japanese troops back to their mainland, all except
the prisoners. Chichi was to be placed in a U.N. Trusteeship
and the island was to be uninhabited for the next twenty

years. Our orders of departure contained the strange request that all livestock on Chichi were to return with us.

The livestock consisted of nineteen horses, numerous pigs, goats, chickens, dogs and one monkey named Hojo. Hojo was a member of Charlie Company. He had joined Charlie during the Bougainville campaign. The Colonel had been using the horses found on the island to whip some of the farmboys into the first and last Marine Corps cavalry outfit. Being a gentleman from Virginia he knew his horses and something about cavalry drills.

The vessel we were to return on was small. The ship was an LST (Landing Ship Tank) mainly used during the war as a landing craft for troops and armor. The ship was three hundred feet in length with a beam of fifty feet and a crew of one-hundred-ten. It was 1,625 tons with a flat bottom. The most striking characteristic was the large doors that made up its bow. When the craft ran up on the beach these huge doors would open, then like a large tongue, a ramp would come out of the open mouth. Tanks and troops would then spew out onto the beach. I give you all these details because in the following yarn the ship is the main character.

We loaded our strange cargo into the hold, and made them as comfortable as we could among the trucks, jeeps, and the rest of our supplies. The situation did not look too promising for our four-legged sailors. We constructed a wooden shack on the main deck to act as a brig for our Japanese prisoners. These men were being taken back to Guam to stand trial for war crimes.

After a day out at sea, the smell of the animals permeated the ship. We were sailing in a dirty barn. It was painful try-ing to sleep between the grunting of the pigs, the barking of the dogs, the baa of the goats and the neighing of the horses. We had a regular Spike Jones band below deck. Chickens were starting to wander around the deck.

The second night out, the ship started taking a beating from a heavy sea. We received the word that a typhoon was about to bear down on us and to secure everything. How do you secure a zoo?

A sailor told me that prior to the ship's arrival at Chichi they had lost their regular captain, who had been transferred to another ship. An inexperienced Executive Officer was now the Acting Captain and the crew did not trust him. The Executive was about to get his baptism of fire.

Within a couple of hours, the wind had increased in force to 070 mph. I recently consulted the U.S. Weather Bureau for the wind speed of that typhoon in that longitude & latitude during late March 1946. They sent me a computer printout, that read, 045, 070, 070, 100, 085, 080, 090, 090. As any old swabbie would tell you, that was a blow and a half.

The ship was being tossed and battered in an honest-to-God typhoon. I stood out on the deck to watch the magnitude and power of the seas. I could actually see the ship bending amidships. The deck plates were continuously crying out in pain. A sailor reassured me that the ship was made to buckle amidships so that it wouldn't snap in half. I felt like crying along with the plates. The ship tipped more then rolled because of its flat bottom. On a good tip you could look UP at the sea. The decks were constantly awash.

WHOOSH!! The brig we made for our prisoners went bottom up and blew over the side, leaving the Japanese still on the deck. We ushered them below deck. Our intentions were to hang them, not drown them. They must have had some fun in that shack while the ship pitched.

We were to be in the typhoon for several days. We were notified that the port on Guam was closed and to ride out the storm as best we could. I had been in rough weather before but nothing like this. The bow would ride high into the air and then come crashing down to bury itself in the sea. Prior to the storm a sailor had informed me that the doors were damaged and had been jury-rigged to stay closed—I prayed they would.

The huge seas controlled our course. The ship appeared helpless, as the helmsman's mettle was being tested, trying to keep the bow into waves in order to keep the ship from broaching. As we left Guam to our stern, the storm increased in velocity. It looked as if we were going to be blown as far south as Truk, in the Caroline Islands. Our brother Regiment, the 21st Marines who were stationed there, might be in for a surprise. I was scared stiff. I wished that I hadn't heard about the doors, or the Executive. I always hated a rough sea, but this was like being in a blender.

As you would expect, our sailors in the hold were taking heavy casualties. A lot of the poor animals, including several horses, had died early on. The dead horses had bloated. The ship reeked from the smell of the dead and the waste of those still alive. This pungent aroma and the ferocity of the storm called for an iron stomach. We were out at sea far longer then we had expected, and therefore had to ration our chow and fresh water, not that anybody had an appetite. Marines and Sailors alike would just lie in their sacks with their head in their helmets. The helmets were strapped to the edge of the sacks and at night, as the ship tipped, you would hear the splashing on the deck, as the helmets run-neth over.

Some Marines volunteered to go into the hold and hoist out the dead horse carcasses through the main hatch. We all watched as the first horse, hogtied, went out of the hold. The horse was bloated to twice its normal size and swinging like a pendulum. Just as the carcass was about to clear the hold, it broke in half, deluging the working party below with horse. The audience fell on the deck laughing. Due to a shortage of volunteers that work detail was canceled.

All day long the carcass of the horse followed in our wake. Was the mangled equine stalking us? It was positively eerie, was it horse or albatross? A blanket of gloom covered the ship.

The following morning our spirits rose as we finally escaped the storm and headed back to Guam; our pursuer had sank beneath the waves. As we entered the harbor we breathed a sigh of relief, but it was much too soon. The Executive was about to dock a ship for the first time. If there is any sort of crosswind, combined with the loss of headway, docking can be a very difficult task for any seaman.

As we bore in, the Marines on board were lining the rail checking out the ships in the harbor. We appeared to be closing on a beautiful yacht, the "Lonely Lady," that was tied up to the pier. The sailors, pointing out its flag, told us it belonged to the Commodore of the island. The yacht was J. P. Morgan class. It was a luxurious show piece made of wood; its polished brass and varnished deck glistened in the sun. The only person on deck was a young officer, waving to us in a friendly manner, a very cool character. This guy seemed real smug; he knew he had it made. He looked like Ensign Pulver, from that play *Mr. Roberts*, a ninety-day wonder, in new, neatly pressed khaki. His demeanor quickly changed to panic as he realized we had lost headway and were being blown into his side. He started making signs with his hands as if to push us off. It was now obvious we were about to mash the "Lonely Lady" against the dock. The guy on the yacht deck had by now completely lost it. He was springing into the air, waving his arms and screaming foul language. We came along broadside and tucked the "Lonely Lady" into the side of the pier.

The Marines were howling with laughter as we watched the polished planks pop and spring into the air. We kissed her, un-puckered, and impolitely continued on our way. We had done extensive damage. We never exchanged a word with the maniac; he was not making any sense. This poor guy was in deep trouble with the Commodore. (Officer of the Deck, what deck?) As we proceeded deeper into the harbor, the sailors were cursing the Executive, and the Marine laughter could not be contained.

We are now heading for a docking space between two other LSTs, who have their doors open onto the beach. Sitting ducks! There is about a thirty-yard space between them.

I figure by now every ship in the harbor had their glasses trained on us and we didn't let them down. The docking operation looked to us as easy as parking a car. I'm sure it appeared that way to the Executive. As we approached the gap between the two ships, we slowed our forward motion and again we lost headway. The crosswind caught our bow, crashing us into the stern of the LST on our starboard side. As we back off, we proceed to cream the other ship on our port side with our stern.

We are on the verge of being wedged between them.

Nobody has the heart to laugh anymore; by now the Marines are bonded to our ship and we are sharing our shipmates' embarrassment. We can no longer even look.

Finally the three crews fight us free and we eventually dock between the ships. Our sailors want to take the ship back out to sea and go down with it. They all agree that it would not be wise to take shore leave. The other two crews are complaining about a horrible smell.

We no longer notice it; we have become the smell. Now comes the *pièce de résistance*. When the ship is made snug to the beach, the Exec gives the order, "Open the bow doors." Sure enough, with all the eyes of Guam staring at us, out of the mouth of our ship comes one hell of a bad breath, followed by the survivors of the typhoon: sick chickens, thin pigs, smelly goats, wild dogs, and a bunch of lame horses. Looking into the hold one can see a bloated horse has commandeered the Colonel's Jeep.

Hojo had been quartered with us, and was in the pink.

I want to know how the heck the Exec got us through that typhoon. I never saw the man. He is now probably living out in Kansas, far from the briny deep.

Next day the headline of the *Guam Daily* read: NOAH'S ARK LANDS ON GUAM.

*"I made it. I owe ya another fifty bucks."*

# ACKNOWLEDGMENTS

In the putting together of *Kilroy Was Here*, there were a few people without whose assistance it could not have been done. My warmest thanks to them: To you, Bill Adler, whose idea it was in the first place. To you, Tom Steele, who dug for buried treasure, found the unfindable, and unscrewed the inscrutable. To you, Will Schwalbe, whose guidance, patience, and encouragement made a book out of it. And, of course, to you, James J. Kilroy, wherever you are.

# PERMISSIONS

Maxene Andrews and Bill Gilbert, excert from *Over Here, Over There.* Copyright 1993 by Maxene Andrews and Bill Gilbert. All rights reserved. Reprinted with the permission of Kensington Publishing Corp.

Richard Armour, "Girdling for War," "Divinity? Fudge!," "End Men," "Brief Case," and "Dead Level" from *Leading with My Left.* Copyright 1945 by Richard Armour. Reprinted with the permission of John Hawkins & Associates, Inc.

Sergeant George Baker, "Sad Sack" cartoon from *The Best from* Yank, *the Army Weekly,* edited by Franklin S. Frosberg. Copyright 1945 by Franklin S. Frosberg. Reprinted with the permission of Dutton, a division of Penguin Putnam Inc.

Staff Sergeant L. A. Brodsky, "Hopeless McGonigle's Brother Wins the DSC" from *The Best from* Yank, *the Army Weekly,* edited by Franklin S. Frosberg. Copyright 1945 by Franklin S. Frosberg. Reprinted with the permission of Dutton, a division of Penguin Putnam Inc.

Cindy Brown, anecdote from "Humor in Uniform" column from www.readersdigest.com. Copyright by The Reader's Digest Assn., Inc. Reprinted with the permission of *Reader's Digest.*

Harry Brown, excerpts from *Artie Greengroin, Pfc.* Copyright 1945 by Harry Brown. Reprinted with the permission of Alfred A. Knopf, a division of Random House, Inc.

Sergeant Irwin Caplan, cartoon from *The Best from* Yank, *the Army Weekly,* edited by Franklin S. Frosberg. Copyright 1945 by Franklin S. Frosberg. Reprinted with the permission of Dutton, a division of Penguin Putnam Inc.

J. F. Carrithers, anecdote from "Humor in Uniform" column in *Reader's Digest.* Copyright by The Reader's Digest Assn., Inc. Reprinted with the permission of *Reader's Digest.*

T.5 James P. Charles, "Furlough Greetings" from *The Best from* Yank, *the Army Weekly,* edited by Franklin S. Frosberg. Copyright 1945 by Franklin S. Frosberg. Reprinted with the permission of Dutton, a division of Penguin Putnam Inc.

Sergeant Ed Cunningham, "Jilted GIs in India Organize First Brush-Off Club" from *The Best from* Yank, *the Army Weekly,* edited by Franklin S. Frosberg. Copyright 1945 by Franklin S. Frosberg. Reprinted with the permission of Dutton, a division of Penguin Putnam Inc.

Corporal Paul E. Deutschmann, "A Sack of Mail" from *The Best from* Yank, *the Army Weekly,* edited by Franklin S. Frosberg. Copyright 1945 by Franklin S. Frosberg. Reprinted with the permission of Dutton, a division of Penguin Putnam Inc.

Private First Class Harold Fleming, "First Epistle to the Selectees" from *The Best from* Yank, *the Army Weekly,* edited by Franklin S. Frosberg. Copyright 1945 by Franklin S. Frosberg. Reprinted with the permission of Dutton, a division of Penguin Putnam Inc.

Sergeant Newton H. Fulbright, "The New York Subway System on the Italian Front" from *The Best from* Yank, *the Army Weekly,* edited by Franklin S. Frosberg. Copyright 1945 by Franklin S. Frosberg. Reprinted with the permission of Dutton, a division of Penguin Putnam Inc.

Marion Hargrove, excerpts from *See Here, Private Hargrove* (New York: Henry Holt, 1942). Copyright 1942 by Marion Hargrove. Reprinted with the permission of the William Morris Agency.

Sergeant Al Hine, "Iran Cooties Share Top Billing with Marx Brothers at the Movies," and "The Invasion of Mae West's Dressing Room" from *The Best from* Yank, *the Army Weekly,* edited by Franklin S. Frosberg. Copyright 1945 by Franklin S. Frosberg. Reprinted with the permission of Dutton, a division of Penguin Putnam Inc.

Bob Hope, excerpt from *I Was There.* Copyright 1994 by Bob Hope Enterprises. Reprinted with the permission of Bob Hope/Hope Enterprises, Inc.

Zyg Jelinski, anecdote from "Humor in Uniform" column in *Reader's Digest.* Copyright by The Reader's Digest Assn., Inc. Reprinted with the permission of *Reader's Digest.*

Ralph G. Martin, excerpts from *The GI War, 1941-1945* (Boston: Little, Brown, 1967). Copyright 1967 by Ralph G. Martin. Reprinted with the permission of Sterling Lord Literistic.

Bill Mauldin, text and cartoons from *Up Front.* Copyright 1945 by Bill Mauldin. Reprinted with the permission of Watkins/Loomis Agency, Inc.

Sergeant Joe McCarthy, "How to Get Lost in a Jungle" from *The Best from* Yank, *the Army Weekly,* edited by Franklin S. Frosberg. Copyright 1945 by Franklin S. Frosberg. Reprinted with the permission of Dutton, a division of Penguin Putnam Inc.

Corporal Bill Monks, "The Ark Lands on Guam." Copyright 1988 by Bill Monks. Reprinted with the permission of Bill Monks.

Corporal James O'Neill, "Nomenclature of the Package, APO" from *The Best from* Yank, *the Army Weekly,* edited by Franklin S. Frosberg. Copyright 1945 by Franklin S. Frosberg. Reprinted with the permission of Dutton, a division of Penguin Putnam Inc.

Private Joe Sims, "The Sergeant" from Ralph G. Martin, *The GI War, 1941-1945* (Boston: Little, Brown, 1967). Copyright 1967 by Ralph G. Martin. Reprinted with the permission of Sterling Lord Literistic.

Corporal Thomas R. St. George, excerpts from *c/o Postmaster.* Copyright 1943 by Thomas R. St. George. Reprinted with the permission of HarperCollins Publishers, Inc.

Sergeant Ralph Stein, "Secret Weapons for the Invasion of Germany" from *The Best from* Yank, *the Army Weekly,* edited by Franklin S. Frosberg. Copyright 1945 by Franklin S. Frosberg. Reprinted with the permission of Dutton, a division of Penguin Putnam Inc.

Tom Tierney, anecdote from "Humor in Uniform" column in *Reader's Digest.* Copyright by The Reader's Digest Assn., Inc. Reprinted with the permission of *Reader's Digest.*

Private Raymond Zauber, "Nomenclature of Whistle, M1" from *The Best from* Yank, *the Army Weekly,* edited by Franklin S. Frosberg. Copyright 1945 by Franklin S. Frosberg. Reprinted with the permission of Dutton, a division of Penguin Putnam Inc.

Ken Zumwalt, excerpt from *The Stars and Stripes: World War II and the Early Years.* Reprinted with the permission of Eakins Press.